SUCCEED IN...

Science

An innovative guide to understanding scientific theories and methods.

Ages 11 – 14

ARCTURUS

ARCTURUS

This edition published in 2014 for Index Books

Copyright © Arcturus Holdings Limited
26/27 Bickels Yard, 151–153 Bermondsey Street,
London SE1 3HA

ISBN: 978-1-84193-219-4
CH000732UK
Supplier 03, Date 1014, Print Run 3899

Printed in China

Contents

Introduction

Succeed in Science is both a guide and exercise book for children and parents who want to improve their knowledge and skills in science.

By the end of this book, students will have sound knowledge of physics, biology and chemistry. This book covers all the essential topics for 11–14 year olds and takes account of all levels of ability. *Succeed in Science* is laid out in a clear, concise way, with each topic explained in easy-to-follow sections to help the reader understand the principles and methods within each field. The book also uses simple, accessible diagrams to explain many scientific principles and describe experiments and reactions.

Each section ends with a number of questions to test the reader's knowledge. These also act as great revision exercises. All the answers are at the back of the book but every reader should be encouraged not to look them up until each question is completed!

By the time the reader has covered each section and all the questions in this book, his or her understanding of the subject will have improved considerably.

What are cells?

All animals and plants are made up out of **cells**. Cells are the building blocks of all living things. Just as a house is made up of bricks, a plant or animal is made up of cells. Cells are often very small and can best be seen with a **microscope**.

Differences between plant and animal cells

There are differences between the cells that make up animals and those of plants. The diagrams below show typical plant and animal cells.

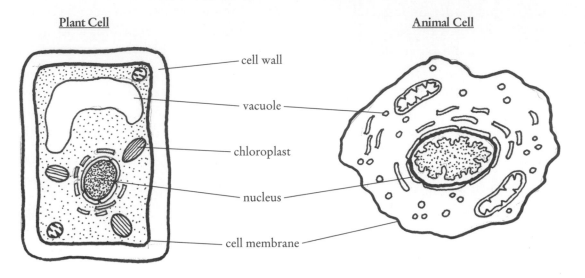

Plant Cell   Animal Cell

- cell wall
- vacuole
- chloroplast
- nucleus
- cell membrane

Animals have a **skeleton** to keep them in shape. The cells of animals are usually soft to the touch.

Plants do not have a skeleton. A plant stays upright because its cells have a tough wall around them.

This cell wall is made from a chemical called **cellulose**.

 KEY FACT: Plant cells have walls around them.
Animal cells do not have walls around them.

More about cells in plants and animals

This table shows the three important parts of all cells and the jobs they do.

Part of the cell	Job
nucleus	stores information and controls the action of the cell
cytoplasm	a mixture of chemicals that includes nutrition that has passed into the cell and waste products on their way out of the cell
cell membrane	holds the cell together and allows nutrients to pass in and waste products to pass out

Some cells, such as mature red blood cells, do not have a nucleus.

Most plant cells also have:

- **chloroplasts** – these contain a green chemical called **chlorophyll** that absorbs energy from the Sun. This energy is needed for the plant to make food.
- a **cell wall** to keep the cell in shape.

Building with cells

There are lots of different types of cell that make up an animal or plant.
A body **organ** such as the heart or a lung has a certain job to do.

Each organ is made up of one or more different types of **tissue**. These are groups of cells that carry out a similar task. The more complex the organ, the more different types of tissue there are.

- Cells of the same type are grouped together to make tissue such as **muscle** or **nerve.**
- All the cells in a tissue carry out a similar task.
- Several different tissues are normally used to make up an **organ.**

Different tissues

Inside your body there are different organs, each with a different job.
An organ is in turn made up of different kinds of tissue.
Some important organs are:

Organ	Tissue in the organ
eye	eye muscle tissue nerve tissue connective tissue (in the white of the eye)
skin	nerve tissue sweat gland tissue blood vessel tissue
heart	lining tissue tendon tissue connective tissue

 KEY FACT: Organs are made of different types of tissue, each of which has a different job to do within the organ.

Specialised cells

Cells in different tissues have different jobs to do.
Their shape helps them to do their job efficiently.

Specialised plant cells

A cell from the **upper surface of a leaf**.
This has lots of chloroplasts to absorb light energy from the Sun.
Cells underneath a leaf have very few chloroplasts.

A **root hair** cell from a plant.
This has no chloroplasts. It is underground and cannot absorb light energy from the Sun.
It has a large surface area so that water and minerals can pass into the cell.

Specialised animal cells

A sperm cell
This is a male sex cell. It needs to swim a long way. It has a tail to propel it and a streamlined shape.

tail

Sperm Cell

nucleus

An egg cell or ovum
This is a female sex cell. It is much bigger than a sperm. It does not have to propel itself.
It does not need the streamlined shape as it only moves slowly.

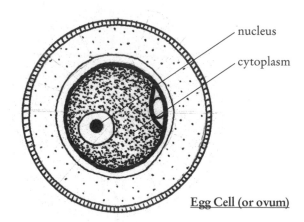

nucleus

cytoplasm

Egg Cell (or ovum)

Cells in the trachea or windpipe
These cells have tiny hairs called **cilia**. The job of these hairs is to trap bacteria and dust so they cannot enter the lungs.

KEY POINT: Specialist cells in plants or animals have been adapted to do special jobs.

Cells

1. John looks at a cell through a microscope. He draws what he can see and labels the diagram.
On his diagram there are the following labels:

nucleus   cell membrane   cytoplasm   vacuole

a. Why do you think this is an animal cell rather than a plant cell?

b. Why is an animal cell easier to squash than a plant cell?

c. Which part of the cell controls the actions of the cell?

d. Why is the cell membrane very thin?

2. **Cells   Organs   Systems   Tissues**
Arrange the four words in the correct order. The first one has been done for you.

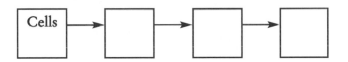

3. a. What is the job of the root hair cell?

   b. How is it adapted for this job?

   c. What is in a leaf cell but not in a root hair cell?

2. Reproduction and Adolescence

Adolescence

Sexual reproduction creates new humans.

In sexual reproduction a male sex cell fuses or joins with a female sex cell to create a new living thing.

Some plants and animals can reproduce without sex. This is called **asexual reproduction**. Asexual reproduction can also be called **cloning**.

For example: a new plant can be grown by taking a cutting from a growing plant.

Before they can reproduce, children need to change into adults. This happens during **adolescence**. This takes place in the early teenage years.

Adolescence in boys

In boys the main changes that take place between the ages of eleven and fourteen are:
- they start to produce male sex cells (**sperm**)
- the voice becomes deeper
- hair grows around the **penis** and on the **scrotum**
- the penis becomes larger.

Adolescence in girls

Adolescence in girls may start earlier, from the age of ten:
- they start to release female sex cells (**ova**) from the **ovaries**
- **breasts** develop
- hair grows around the **vulva**, the fleshy external opening to the **vagina**
- a regular **menstrual cycle** begins, with **periods** each month
- hips broaden, ready for childbirth.

Other changes in boys and girls

Both boys and girls change emotionally during adolescence.
They become sexually attracted to other people.
They become much more interested in their appearance and what other people think about them.

How are these changes controlled?

The changes that take place in both boys and girls during adolescence are controlled by special chemicals called **hormones**.
In boys they are controlled by the hormone **testosterone**. This is produced by cells in the testes.
In girls they are controlled by the hormone **oestrogen**. This is produced in the ovaries.

Menstruation

A period is a result of the uterus, or womb, preparing itself each month to receive a fertilised egg.

The diagram below shows the main parts of the female reproductive system.

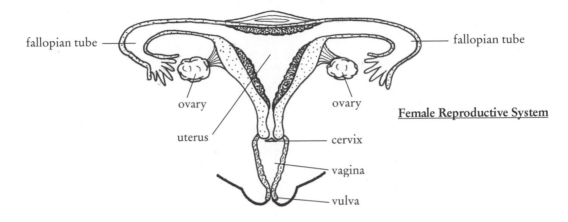

Female Reproductive System

In the menstrual cycle:
- an egg ripens and is released from an ovary each month
- as the egg travels slowly along the fallopian tube, the lining of the uterus thickens
- if the egg enters the uterus unfertilised the thickened lining falls away
- the unfertilised egg and the lining of the uterus pass out through the vagina. This is the period.

Stages in the menstrual cycle

This diagram shows the changes that take place during the menstrual cycle.

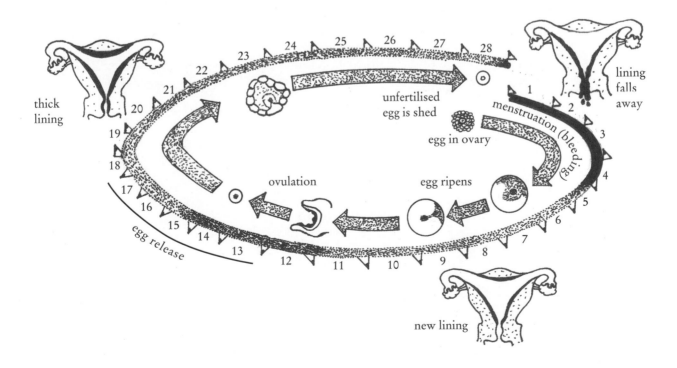

The changes in the menstrual cycle are controlled by **hormones.**
- **Oestrogen** – this causes the lining to thicken.
- **Progesterone** – this maintains the thickened lining of the uterus.

The most likely time for an egg to be fertilised is between 15 and 22 days.
If fertilisation takes place, the menstrual cycle stops while the egg develops.
If fertilisation does not take place menstruation occurs and the thickened lining of the uterus is lost through the vagina.

 KEY FACT: Scientists are now able to **clone** some animals. This means they can produce an animal which is an exact copy of its parent.

? ? ? ? Questions ? ? ? ?

1. What is meant by *asexual reproduction*?

2. Which cells fuse together in sexual reproduction?

3. Describe the changes that take place to the sex organs of a boy during adolescence.

4. Explain why some plants can reproduce asexually but humans cannot.

5. Look at the diagram of the female reproductive system on page 11.
   Use words on the diagram to answer the following questions.

   a. Which part of the female reproductive system is the entrance to the uterus from the vagina?

   b. Which part of the female reproductive system releases eggs?

   c. Which part of the female reproductive system prepares itself to receive a fertilised egg?

6. Look at the diagram of the menstrual cycle on page 11. Use it to answer the following questions.

   a. What is the length of the menstrual cycle?

   b. What happens between the 7th and 10th days of the cycle?

   c. Where does this happen?

   d. Between which days is an egg released from an ovary?

   e. What is happening between days 16 and 20 of the cycle?

7. What is menstruation?

3. Fertilisation

The diagram below shows the main parts of the male reproductive system.

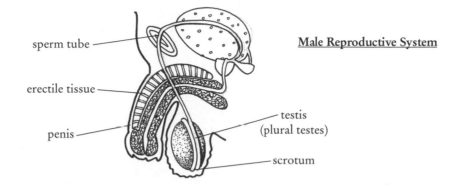

Male Reproductive System

sperm tube

erectile tissue

penis

testis (plural testes)

scrotum

During **sexual intercourse**:
- the **erectile tissue** becomes filled with blood, causing the penis to swell and become **erect**
- the penis is inserted into the vagina
- sperm from the **testes** flows through the sperm tube and out through the end of the penis
- the sperm are normally released at the **cervix**, the entrance to the uterus.

The sperm swim through the uterus and along the fallopian tubes. If they meet an egg in the fallopian tubes, **fertilisation** may take place.

Fertilisation is the joining together, or **fusion**, of a male sex cell (sperm) and a female sex cell (ovum or egg).

When an egg is fertilised, one sperm enters the egg and the nuclei of the two cells join together. From this single cell a new human is formed. The nucleus of this cell contains information from both the mother and the father.

The diagram below shows what happens when fertilisation takes place.

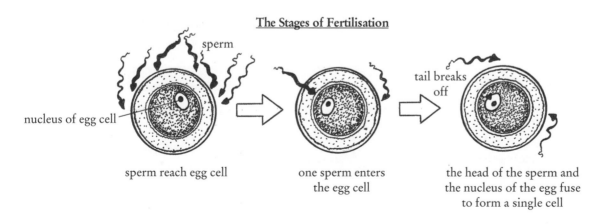

The Stages of Fertilisation

sperm

nucleus of egg cell

tail breaks off

sperm reach egg cell

one sperm enters the egg cell

the head of the sperm and the nucleus of the egg fuse to form a single cell

KEY FACT: Fertilisation occurs when a male sex cell fuses with a female sex cell. It takes place in plants and animals.

13

From embryo to fetus

The developing fetus

The single cell is produced when the sperm and egg cell fuse then divide. These cells then divide several times as they travel along the fallopian tube to the uterus. This is now called an **embryo**.

The embryo travels to the uterus and beds itself in the lining. Here the embryo develops into a **fetus**.
The embryo becomes a fetus when it has recognisable human features.
The fetus:
- is joined to the **placenta** by the **umbilical cord**
- is surrounded by a watery liquid that keeps it warm and protects it from shock.

Food, oxygen and waste materials pass along the umbilical cord.

The diagram below shows the fetus developing inside the mother.

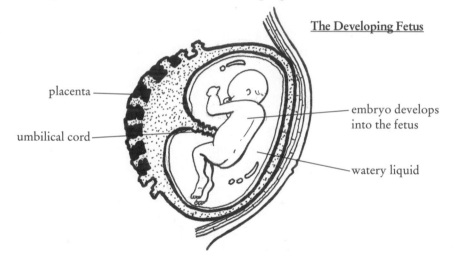

The Developing Fetus

placenta

umbilical cord

embryo develops into the fetus

watery liquid

It is important to remember that the blood of the fetus and that of the mother never mix.

After nine months of **pregnancy**, the baby is born through the vagina. A human baby is helpless at birth and relies on care from parents if it is to survive.

? ? ? ? Questions ? ? ? ?

1. A frog produces hundreds of eggs in a pond but a human female produces only one egg each month. Explain this difference.

2. What is the difference between a fetus and an embryo?

3. a. Which organs produce **i.** sperm and **ii.** eggs?

    b. What name is given to the process where sperm cells and egg cells are fused or joined together?

    c. How many new cells are made when a sperm cell and an egg cell fuse?

4. State two reasons why the embryo is surrounded by a watery fluid.

4. Feeding Relationships/Habitats

The place where a particular plant or animal lives is called its **habitat**.

A **habitat** is a community of plants and animals that depend on each other.
A habitat provides:
- food
- shelter
- a place to reproduce.

In a large garden there can be a number of different habitats. Possible habitats in the garden could be a tree, a hedge, an area of nettles or a bed of flowers.

A hedge can provide:
- food for worms and other soil-based animals that feed on the dead leaves
- shelter for birds and hedgehogs.

Adaptation

Animals in any habitat have special features that enable them to live there.
To live in a pond a fish needs:
- fins
- a tail
- gills.

To live in the wild a fox needs:
- strong hind legs so that it can run fast to overtake its prey
- canine teeth to tear flesh when it feeds
- lungs for gas exchange.

Plants are also adapted to suit their habitat. Woodland plants often develop and flower in the spring when light can penetrate through the trees. In summer, when there is little light, they are dormant.

The plants in a pond grow most in summer when there is plenty of sunlight.
This gives them energy for making food and growth.
They are adapted to absorb energy from the Sun by floating on the water or having long stems so that their leaves are close to the water surface.

Feeding

Plants can make their own food by the process of **photosynthesis**.
Animals cannot make their own food. They have to eat either plants or other animals.

Plants use **carbon dioxide** from the air and **water** from the soil to make food.
They make a simple sugar called **glucose**.
This is then converted into **starch** which can be stored.

Plants that make their own food are called **producers**.
Animals such as worms and slugs that feed directly from plants are called **primary consumers**.
Animals that eat primary consumers are called **secondary consumers**.
Animals that eat secondary consumers are called **tertiary consumers**.

These feeding relationships can be summarised in a **food chain**.

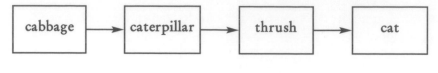

| cabbage | → | caterpillar | → | thrush | → | cat |

producer   primary consumer   secondary consumer   tertiary consumer

Food webs

A food chain summarises the feeding relationships of a number of organisms.
Looking at the food chain above you might not realise that a thrush may eat other food than caterpillars (e.g. worms) and will be eaten by other animals than cats.
The situation is more complicated and is better summarised by a **food web**.
This consists of a number of food chains.

<u>A Food Web Based On The Oak Tree</u>

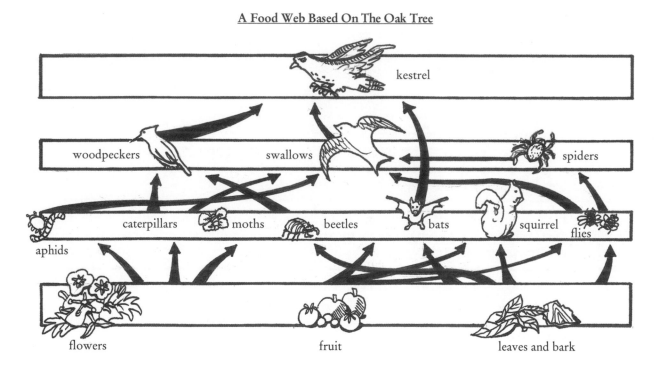

Changes in the environment

If you look at a habitat such as a hedge or a tree in a garden over a period of time you will see that changes are continually taking place.
Each day there are changes in the:
- light intensity
- temperature
- moisture level.

During a year there are even greater variations in all these factors.
These changes can affect:
- the number of organisms in a habitat
- the type of organisms in a habitat
- the activity of the organisms in a habitat.

Survival

To survive in a changing habitat, organisms need to be adapted to cope with the extreme conditions.

The tree loses its leaves in winter to reduce the loss of heat and water – it may not be able to take in water if the ground is frozen.

Some animals may hibernate during the winter.

Insects burrow into the ground or leaf litter, and their offspring survive the winter as eggs.

 KEY FACT: A habitat supports a variety of plants and animals that depend on each other.

? ? ? ? Questions ? ? ? ?

1. What is a habitat?

2. State three things that a habitat must provide.

3. a. A garden pond provides a habitat for fish. What is needed for fish to survive in the habitat?

   b. Describe and explain three ways a fish is adapted to live in a pond.

4. Look at the food web on page 16. Write three food chains with flowers as the producer.
   flowers →
   flowers →
   flowers →

5. What two substances are needed for plants to be able to make food?

6. A herbivore is an animal that feeds off plants. A carnivore feeds off other animals. An omnivore can eat plants or animals.
   Classify each of the following as a herbivore, carnivore or omnivore.
   a. Spider
   b. Aphid
   c. Human being

7. Bluebells are woodland plants. Explain why they grow and flower in spring.

8. State two ways in which a water lily plant that grows in a pond is adapted to absorb energy from the Sun.

5. Variation and Classification

Variation

Human beings are a **species**, which is a type of organism.
This table summarises some of the similarities and some of the differences between human beings.

Similarities	Differences
a head, two arms and two legs	height
walking on two legs	weight
breathing with their lungs	hair, skin and eye colour

The differences between species and between individuals of a species is called **variation**.

Genetics

The **genetic** information you inherit from your parents determines what you are.
It is stored in the nuclei of your cells. It came from the egg cell and sperm that fused when you were created.
This information determines:
- your sex – whether you are male or female
- the natural colour of your hair
- the colour of your eyes.

This genetic information can also determine your height, body shape and weight.
However, these are also influenced by **environmental factors** such as:
- what you eat
- how much exercise you take.

Other things about your appearance are totally controlled by environmental factors.
These include:
- hair length
- whether you wear an earring
- the length of finger nails.

Most of the differences between human beings are due to a combination of genetic and environmental factors.

Classification

Scientists **classify** species of organisms into groups. This is needed because there are well over a million different organisms known.
There are four **kingdoms** or groups of organisms.

Variation and Classification

Kingdom	Characteristic
plants	many cells and make their own food
animals	many cells and have senses, nerves and muscles
fungi	do not have cells: digest food outside the body
protists	single-celled organisms

Classes of animals

Animals are classified as **vertebrates** (animals with backbones) or **invertebrates** (animals without backbones). The different groups of vertebrates and invertebrates are shown in the diagram below.

The numbers by each group give the approximate number of known species.

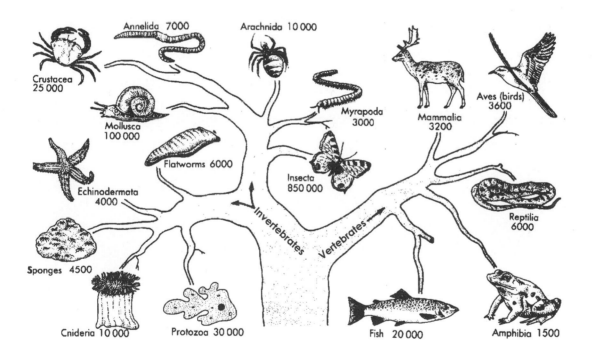

KEY POINT: You do not need to remember the different groups of animals, but you do need to be able to group animals according to their physical appearance.

Learn the characteristics of each group of vertebrates.

? ? ? ? Questions ? ? ? ?

1. Explain whether skin colour is determined by genetic factors, environmental factors or both.

2. Here is a list of animals
   frog   goldfish   monkey   starfish   sparrow   worm
   Which of these are vertebrates?

3. What is the difference between vertebrates and invertebrates?

4. To which group of invertebrates do snails belong?

5. State one difference between species in the groups Mammalia and Aves.

6. State one similarity between species in the groups Fish and Amphibia.

6. Acids and Alkalis

Acids

What do you taste as you bite into a green apple?
You taste a sour taste. The sour taste is due to acid in the apple.

Acids are also found in lemons, oranges and limes. These are called citrus fruits and the acid is **citric acid**. Vinegar tastes sour because it contains **ethanoic acid**.

Three common acids used in the laboratory are:
Sulphuric acid H_2SO_4
Nitric acid HNO_3
Hydrochloric acid HCl
They are sometimes called **mineral acids**.

Alkalis

Alkalis are often soapy to touch. They are the opposite of acids.
Common alkalis in the home are found in bicarbonate of soda, washing powders and washing soda.

Four common alkalis used in the laboratory are:
Sodium hydroxide $NaOH$ (sometimes called caustic soda)
Potassium hydroxide KOH
Calcium hydroxide $Ca(OH)_2$
Ammonia NH_3

Water is neither an acid nor an alkali. Water is **neutral**.

Tests for acids and alkalis

1. Litmus paper

Litmus is a type of moss. A solution of the colouring matter in the moss can be used to detect acids and alkalis.
If a few drops are added to an acid the solution turns RED.
If a few drops are added to an alkali the solution turns BLUE.

ACID = RED

ALKALI = BLUE

Litmus paper is paper which has been soaked in litmus solution and dried. It is useful for testing for acids or alkalis.

2. Universal indicator

Universal indicator is a mixture of dyes. It changes colour a number of times and from the colour the pH value of the solution can be found.

pH is a number on a scale (usually 0–14) which shows how acidic or alkaline a substance is. pH values less than 7 show acidity. (The lower the value the stronger the acid.)

pH value of exactly 7 shows neutral.
pH value greater than 7 shows alkalinity. (The higher the value the stronger the alkali.)

3. pH meter

A **pH meter** is a simple machine that will find the pH straight away. A probe is put into the substance being tested. The pH value is shown on a scale or on a digital display.

Neutralisation

A **neutralisation** reaction involves an **acid** and a **base or alkali**.
One of the products of neutralisation is always **water**.

Examples of neutralisation

1. Acids in digestion

Hydrochloric acid in your stomach is used in the digestion of food. Minor problems of indigestion are caused by too much acid in the stomach. This excess acid can be neutralised by adding a weak alkali. This is called an **antacid**.
Suitable antacids are **milk of magnesia** (a suspension of magnesium hydroxide) and **bicarbonate of soda** (sodium hydrogencarbonate).

2. The acidity of soils

If soil becomes too acidic the yield of crops is reduced. Rain and artificial fertilisers make the soil more acidic. The excess acidity can be treated with **lime (calcium hydroxide)**.

3. Wasp and bee stings

Wasp and bee stings are treated in different ways. A wasp sting is treated by adding **vinegar (a weak acid)**. A bee sting is treated using **bicarbonate of soda (an alkali)**. In both cases the remedy neutralises the sting.

4. Removing acidic gases from gases leaving power stations

Coal-fired power stations can produce sulphur dioxide. This gas can be dangerous. It is an acidic gas. It can be removed by passing it over limestone. The **limestone (calcium carbonate)** neutralises the acidic gas.

KEY FACT: Remember that an acid is needed to neutralise an alkali and an alkali to neutralise an acid.

Acids and Alkalis

1. Explain why wasp and bee stings are treated in different ways.

2. Antacids are often in the form of tablets. Suggest one advantage of tablets rather than powder.

3. You are given three liquids: water, dilute hydrochloric acid and sodium hydroxide solution. How could you use pieces of red and blue litmus paper to tell which liquid is which?

4. You are given a bottle of lithium hydroxide solution. Would you expect this to be acidic, alkaline or neutral? Explain your choice.

5. A solution of hydrochloric acid has a pH value of 1.
   a. Which of the following could neutralise this solution?

      bicarbonate of soda   **lemon juice**   **sodium hydroxide**   **sulphuric acid**   **water**

   b. What would be the pH value of a neutral solution?

   c. Which element is present in all acids?

6. Tim wants to find which of two different brands of antacid tablet contains more alkali.
   He measures out 25 cm³ samples of acid into two beakers.
   He drops tablets of Brand A into one beaker and tablets of Brand B into the other.
   He keeps doing this until the solutions stop fizzing.
   How could he tell which antacid, A or B, contains more alkali?

7. Jenny drops some sulphuric acid onto the floor. How should she clean it up?

Scientists are always striving to produce new materials with better properties than existing materials.

Recently a plastic material has been made which conducts electricity. Could this, one day, replace copper wires in electrical circuits? Copper is becoming expensive as amounts in the Earth are limited. A plastic would be easier to make into a wire and would be much lighter.

New materials are made as a result of **chemical reactions**.
During a chemical reaction a **chemical change** takes place.
It is impossible to reverse a chemical change.
A change that can be reversed is called a **physical change**.

Ice melts to form water. This is a physical change because the reverse change takes place when water is placed in a freezer and ice forms.

Chemical change is sometimes called **permanent change** and physical change is called **temporary change**.

Using acids to make new materials

Acids can be used to make new materials.

1. from metals

Many metals will react with dilute acids to produce hydrogen gas.

If a piece of magnesium metal is added to dilute hydrochloric acid, bubbles of colourless **hydrogen** gas are seen. This reaction can be summarised in a **word equation** as:

magnesium + hydrochloric acid → magnesium chloride + hydrogen

If a **lighted splint** is held close to the mouth of the test tube, the hydrogen gas burns with a **squeaky pop**.

2. from carbonates (e.g. limestone)

A carbonate reacts with a dilute acid to form **carbon dioxide** gas.

If some calcium carbonate is added to dilute hydrochloric acid, bubbles of colourless carbon dioxide gas are seen. This reaction can be summarised in a **word equation** as:

calcium carbonate + hydrochloric acid → calcium chloride + water + carbon dioxide

The gas is bubbled through colourless **limewater** solution. The solution goes **cloudy white** (like milk).

Burning

Burning or **combustion** is a chemical reaction which produces new materials.
In doing this it also releases energy.

When a substance burns it uses up oxygen and forms one or more **oxides**.

Some substances burn and others do not.
A substance that burns, e.g. wood, is said to be **combustible**.

A substance that catches light easily is said to be **flammable.**
Substances that are flammable sometimes have a hazard warning sign on them.

Metals that burn

Some metals burn to form a metal oxide.

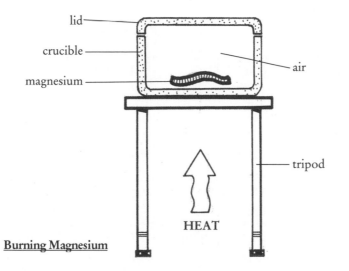

Burning Magnesium

When magnesium is heated in air, the magnesium burns with a bright white flame.
The white ash remaining is called **magnesium oxide.**
The reaction can be summarised in a **word equation** as:

magnesium + oxygen → magnesium oxide

? ? ? ? Questions ? ? ? ?

1. Is each of the following changes a chemical change or a physical change?
   a. The burning of paper.
   b. Dissolving salt in water.
   c. Baking bread.
   d. Boiling water.
   e. Drying washing.
2. When a glass beaker is placed over a burning candle, the candle continues to burn for a while and then goes out.
   a. Explain why this happens.
   b. How would it be different if a larger beaker was used?
3. Three hundred years ago scientists believed that when a substance burns its mass decreases. Explain why we now know that the mass of a metal such as magnesium increases when it burns.
4. Complete the following word equations for reactions that produce new materials.
   a. Magnesium + sulphuric acid → magnesium sulphate + _____
   b. Zinc carbonate + hydrochloric acid → zinc chloride + water + _____
   c. Calcium + oxygen → _____
   d. Iron + _____ → iron chloride + _____
   e. Sodium carbonate + _____ → sodium sulphate + _____
      + _____

8. States of Matter

All substances can exist in three states of matter depending upon conditions of temperature and pressure.

These are **solid**, **liquid** and **gas**.

The temperature at which a solid turns to a liquid is called the **melting point** (the opposite is the **freezing point**).

The temperature at which a liquid turns to a gas is called the **boiling point**.

The properties of solids, liquids and gases are shown in the table below.

Property	Solid	Liquid	Gas
volume	definite	definite	fills whole container
shape	definite	shape of bottom of container	shape of whole container
density	high	medium	low
ease of flow	does not flow unless powdered	flows easily	flows easily
expansion on heating	low	medium	high
compression	very low	low	high

Changes of state

This diagram shows how the three states of matter can be changed.

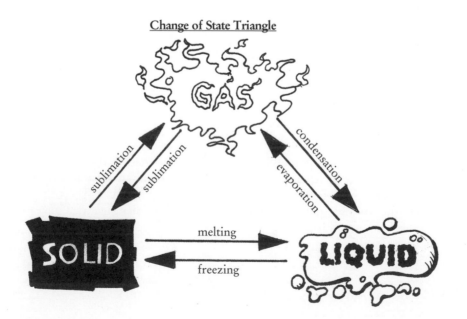

Change of State Triangle

26

Particle model of solids, liquids and gases

Solids, liquids and gases are made up of very tiny particles.
The diagram below shows how these particles are arranged in a solid, a liquid and a gas.

<u>Particles in a Solid, a Liquid and a Gas</u>

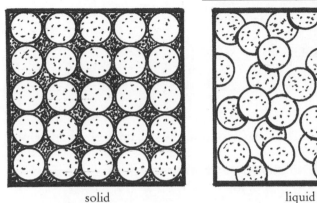

solid   liquid   gas

This table summarises how the particles are arranged and move in solids, liquids and gases.

State	Arrangement of particles	Movement of particles
solid	particles closely packed together	little movement – only vibrations
liquid	particles close together but not regularly arranged	particles have some movement
gas	particles widely spaced	particles moving rapidly in all directions

? ? ? ? Questions ? ? ? ?

1. Water can exist in three states of matter. What are these three states and under what conditions of temperature do they exist?

2. Here is some information about bromine.

Bromine

melting point   -7.2°C
boiling point   59°C

  a. In which state, solid, liquid or gas, is bromine at room temperature (20°C)?
  b. What would happen if some bromine was put in a freezer at -10°C?

3. a. In which state are particles most widely spaced?
   b. In which state are particles regularly arranged?
   c. In which state are the particles moving fastest?

27

9. Separating Mixtures

Many materials consist of mixtures of substances. Scientists often want to separate mixtures and produce **pure** substances.

Separating a mixture of salt and sand in rock salt

Key words
salt – **solute**
water – **solvent**
mixture of salt and
water – **solution**

Rock salt is a mixture of salt and sand.
The rock is crushed and the mixture is added to water.
The salt **dissolves** but the sand does not.
The resulting mixture is called a salt **solution**.

When the solution is poured through a filter, the salt solution passes through the filter paper but the sand does not.

The diagram below shows how sand can be separated from the salt solution by **filtering**.

The salt can be recovered from the salt solution by **evaporation**.
The apparatus in the diagram shows how evaporation can be done.

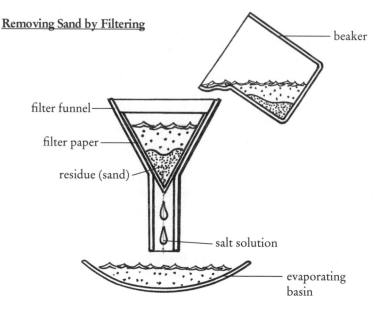

Removing Sand by Filtering

beaker

filter funnel

filter paper

residue (sand)

salt solution

evaporating basin

Separating water from sea water (salt solution)

In many countries there is a shortage of suitable water to use for household supplies.
In such places water may be made from sea water, which is a salt solution.
This can be done by a process called **distillation**.

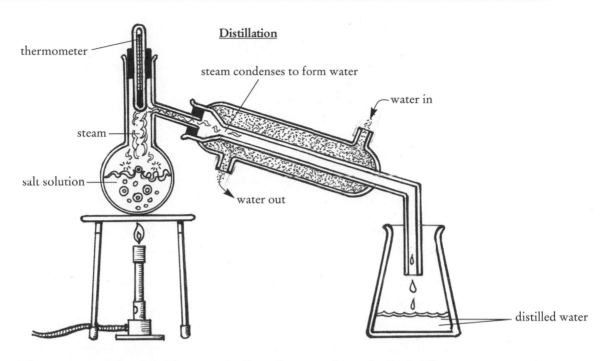

Distillation

The sea water is heated. The water boils and escapes from the flask. The steam escapes into the condenser. Here the steam **condenses** and forms liquid water.
This is collected in the receiver.
Distillation can be thought of as **evaporation** followed by **condensation**.
The impurities, salt in this case, remain in the flask.

Separating mixtures of dyes

Many processed foods are coloured by artificial dyes.
The mixtures of dyes in a food dissolved in water can be separated by **chromatography**.
A drop of the solution containing a mixture of dissolved substances is placed at the bottom of a piece of filter paper. This is dipped into water and left. Water rises up the filter paper and the different dissolved substances separate at different rates. Each different substance forms a spot on the filter paper.

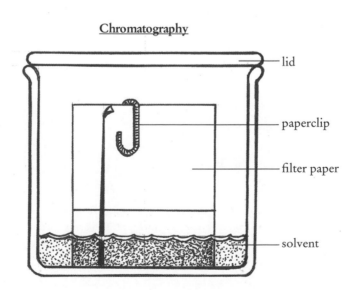

Chromatography

On the piece of filter paper, called a **chromatogram**, you can see the results obtained with three dyes A, B and C (see diagram opposite).

There is also a mixture of dyes X. From the results it can be concluded that:

- X is a mixture of two dyes because there are two spots on the chromatogram
- X contains dye B and dye C but not dye A. X has two spots – one at the same height as dye B and one at the same height as dye C.

Separating miscible liquids

Crude oil is made up from a complex mixture of miscible liquids.

It is possible to separate crude oil into saleable products but not pure compounds by **fractional distillation**.

Key words
liquids that mix completely e.g. ethanol and water – **miscible** liquids that do not mix e.g. paraffin and water – **immiscible**

Hexane and methylbenzene are a pair of miscible liquids that can be separated by fractional distillation. When a mixture of hexane and methylbenzene are heated, hexane (boiling point 69°C) boils off before methylbenzene (boiling point 111°C).

This diagram shows the apparatus used to separate hexane and methylbenzene by fractional distillation.

Fractional Distillation

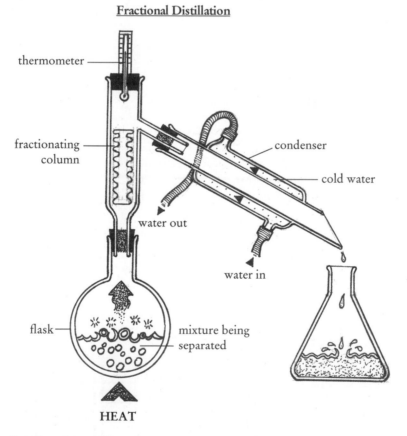

thermometer

fractionating column

condenser

cold water

water out

water in

flask

mixture being separated

HEAT

The first fraction collected up to 69°C is mainly hexane.

The second fraction between 69°C and 111°C is a mixture of hexane and methylbenzene.

The third fraction boiling above 111°C is mainly methylbenzene.

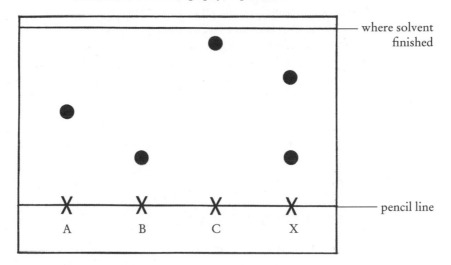

Results of a Chromatography Experiment

1. Look at the chromatogram above.
   a. If a mixture of A, B and C is made, how many spots would this produce on a similar chromatogram?

   b. If a mixture of X and C is made, how many spots would this produce on a similar chromatogram?

   c. Why is it important to use a pencil line rather than a pen line?

2. Two miscible liquids have boiling points of 101°C and 103°C. Why would it be difficult to separate these liquids by fractional distillation?

10. Fuels and Energy

Where does our energy come from?

Energy is needed to:
- make things **move**
- **heat** our living space
- **light** the areas where we live and work.

Electricity provides much of the energy that we need each day.
Most of our electricity is generated by burning a **fuel**.
Common fuels include wood, gas, coal and oil.
Of these, wood is easy to replace as more trees can be grown. It is called a **replaceable fuel**.
Coal, oil and natural gas are **fossil fuels.**
Governments are planning to produce more electricity from wind, solar power and tidal power.

Fossil fuels took millions of years to form and cannot be replaced.
Burning fossil fuels releases gases such as carbon dioxide, sulphur dioxide and nitrogen oxides.

How long will coal and oil last?

Fossil fuels are being used up rapidly.
- The UK has enough coal to last for two hundred years.
- The known reserves of gas and oil will not last as long as coal. They are having to be imported.
- Our use of gas, oil and coal needs to be as efficient as possible.
- We need to find alternative sources of energy for transport and for generating electricity.

Measuring energy

When a gas or electricity bill arrives at home, the cost is for the energy transferred through the gas pipes or electricity cables.
Energy is measured in joules (J).
One **joule** is a very small amount of energy.
It is the amount of energy that leaves your body when you lift a 1 kg bag of sugar through a height of 1 metre.

To boil a kettle of water from cold needs about 600 000 J of energy. The amount of energy needed to heat enough water to fill a bath will be a very large number.
Other units we use are:

> **kilojoules** (kJ)   1 kJ = 1 000J
> **megajoules**(mJ)   1 mJ = 1 000 000J

Fuels and Energy

Renewable resources

What is a renewable resource?

A renewable energy resource is one that will not run out during the lifetime of the Earth.

Plants are renewable energy resources. They are renewable because we can grow fresh crops each year. Energy from plants is known as **biomass**. Other renewable resources include:
- wind
- waves and tides
- moving water
- the Sun
- geothermal energy.

Moving air and water

Energy from the Sun makes the **wind** blow. The energy in moving air can be used to turn wind turbines and generate electricity. These can be built singly or in groups, called wind farms.

The sea provides two important energy resources: **waves** and **tides**. Waves are caused by the wind, and tides are due mainly to the effect of the Moon pulling on the oceans.

Energy from tides is reliable, as it depends only on the Moon going round the Earth.

Electricity generated from **moving water** in fast-flowing rivers and streams is called **hydroelectricity**. Its energy source is the Sun, which causes the evaporation of water from the sea.

Solar energy

Energy from the Sun is used directly in three different ways:
- it is used to grow crops
- it can be used to heat water
- it can be used to generate electricity.

In some countries, hot-water tanks on the roofs of houses are a common sight. Energy from the Sun is used to heat water as it passes through copper pipes.

Solar cells use energy from the Sun to produce electricity. They are expensive to make and they only produce electricity in daylight. They are useful to power calculators, which only use a small amount of electricity.

Solar cells are used by satellites and spacecraft to generate electricity. They have vast panels of cells to generate enough electricity for the on-board computers and other devices. They store surplus energy in batteries so that they have a reserve supply.

Geothermal energy is the energy in hot rocks below the Earth's surface. The energy in the rocks is used to heat water. If the rocks are hot enough, they can be used to generate steam to drive a turbine and produce electricity.

? ? ? ? Questions ? ? ? ?

1. A block of metal weighs 100 kg. It is being lifted 5 m.
   How much energy is required to do this?

2. What are the advantages of generating electricity from renewable sources rather than
   burning fossil fuels such as coal?

3. Little electricity is generated from solar power. Suggest reasons for this.

4. What causes a. waves; b. tides?

5. Water runs down from a lake through a turbine. Water can also be pumped back up to
   the lake.
   a. What name is given to electricity generated from water moving through a turbine?

   b. At some times of the day more electricity is generated than is necessary.
      i. Suggest how this electricity could be used.
      ii. What is the advantage of doing this?

11. Electricity

Current in circuits

To light a lamp using a power supply (cell or a low-voltage power pack), there needs to be a complete route from the power supply to the lamp and back again. This route is called a **circuit**.

In a circuit there is a complete current path from the positive terminal of the power supply to the negative terminal.

If there is a break in the circuit, the lamp goes out.

A circuit with a break in it can be used to test which materials are **conductors** and which are **insulators**.

A gap in a circuit can be used as a switch:

- If the gap is closed using a conducting material, the circuit is switched on.
- The circuit is switched off when the gap is open.

The diagram below uses circuit symbols to show a lamp that can be switched on and off.

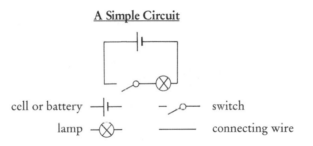

A Simple Circuit

cell or battery ———⊣⊢——   —•⧀•— switch

lamp —⊗—   ——— connecting wire

Series and parallel circuits

Two lamps and a cell can be connected in two different ways:

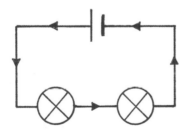
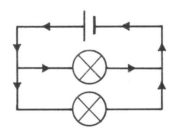

series circuit e.g. Christmas tree lights   parallel circuit e.g. most household circuits

The current from the cell passes through each lamp in turn, one after the other.

The current splits at the junction before the lamps and rejoins at the junction after the lamps.

Measuring electric current

A lamp in a circuit that is lit shows that an electric current is passing.

An ammeter is a meter that measures the size of an electric current in **amps** (A). Ammeters are always connected in series in a circuit.

Ammeters can be either digital, which are easy to read, or analogue, which involve a needle moving over a scale.

Analogue meters call for more care when taking readings, as you have to interpret the scale divisions and make judgements about readings between scale divisions.

Ammeter Measuring the Current Passing Through a Lamp

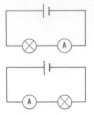

Energy transfer

If we look at the two circuits we see that in one the current entering the lamp is being measured. In the other the current leaving the lamp is being measured. In fact the two ammeter readings are the same ; the lamps have not used any current. The current is the same at all points in a series circuit.

This may seem strange, because without a current the lamp does not work, so how does a lamp produce light?
- What comes out of a lamp is **energy**, in the form of heat and light.
- The current in a circuit transfers energy from the source, the battery or power supply, to the lamp and other components such as motors or heaters.

Energy is transferred around a circuit by moving charged particles.
In metals the moving particles are electrons; these carry a negative charge.
Electrons cannot move in an **insulator** but they are free to move around in a **conductor**.
The electron movement is from negative to positive, even though we always mark current directions as being from positive to negative.

Controlling the current

The brighter the lamp, the greater the current passing through it.
The current can be made bigger or smaller if a **variable resistor** is included in the circuit.

A variable resistor works by changing the **resistance** in a circuit; the more resistance there is, the smaller the current that passes.

The diagram below shows a variable resistor and how it can be set up within a lamp dimming circuit.

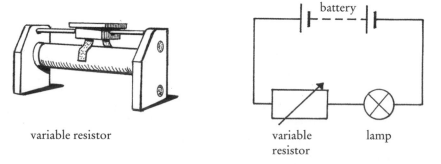

variable resistor   variable   lamp
                                     resistor

Moving the slider to one end of the variable resistor makes the lamp light at its brightest. The lamp is dimmest when the slider is moved to the opposite end.
Variable resistors can control other things besides lamps. They act as the volume control on radios and they can also be used to control the speed of an electric motor.

Changing the current

The size of the current that passes in a circuit depends on:
- the **voltage** of the current source
- the **resistance** of the circuit.

A variable resistor changes the resistance in the circuit. This then changes the current passing.

Increase the voltage that drives the current in a circuit and the charge travels round the circuit at a greater rate. This increases the current.

When you add more lamps in a series circuit, the current becomes less because you are increasing the circuit resistance.

Adding more lamps in parallel causes more current in the circuit because there are more routes available for the current to pass through.

When the current splits at a junction:
- the sum of the currents along the branches is equal to the current from the power supply
- the current that passes into a junction is equal to the current that passes out.

? ? ? ? Questions ? ? ? ?

1. Put a ring around the materials that do not conduct electricity.
   aluminium brass copper nylon polythene steel

2. Which type of circuit, series or parallel, has only one conducting path?

3. In which type of circuit does the current split and rejoin at junctions?

4. The diagrams below show two different ways of connecting the lights in two bedrooms in a house.

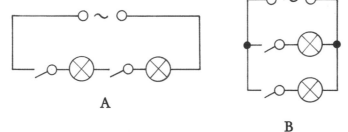

A

B

   a.Which circuit should be used?
b. Explain why this circuit should be used.

5. A current of 2 A passes into the filament of a lamp.
   a. How much current passes out of the filament?
   b. How much current does the lamp use up?

6. What is the job of the current in a circuit?

7. State two types of energy emitted by a lamp that is switched on.

8. This diagram shows a variable resistor connected in series with a battery and a motor.

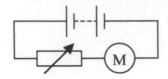

  a. What type of circuit is shown, series or parallel?
  b. Describe what the circuit is able to do.

9. The diagram shows three identical lamps connected to a battery.

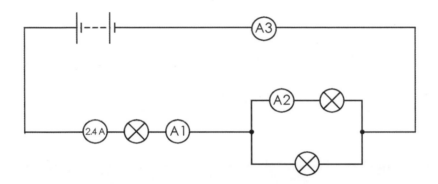

Write down the readings on ammeters A1, A2 and A3.

A1 _____; A2 _____; A3 _____

12. Forces and their Effects

What do forces do?

Forces can
- start and stop things from moving
- cause changes in direction
- change the shape of things when they squash or bend or stretch or twist them.

Forces are described by a phrase such as **object A pulls or pushes object B.**

Forces on a diagram are shown by an arrow in the direction of the push or pull. The larger the arrow the bigger the force.

Examples

The Earth pulls the Moon	The man pushes the pram
The Earth, like all other very massive objects, pulls everything else towards it.	

Forces are measured in **Newtons** (N for short).
Weight is a force.
On the Earth the weight of each kilogram of material is about 10 N.
A 50 kg bag of cement is pulled towards the Earth with a force of 500 N.

Staying still

Many things around us are stationary (not moving) even though there are forces acting on them. Everything on the Earth has at least one force acting on it – the Earth's pull.
If something is not moving there must also be another force pushing or pulling it so that the forces are **balanced**. When you stand on the ground there is an upward force that balances the downward pull of the Earth. There are two equal-sized forces acting on you in opposite directions. The forces on you are balanced.

Floating and sinking

- If you push a plastic ball into a bucket of water you can feel the water pushing it back up – the more you push it in, the bigger the upward push of the water becomes.
- When a ball **floats** the forces on it are balanced; the upward push of the water is equal in size to the downward pull of the Earth.
- An object **sinks** if its weight is greater than the upward push of the water.

KEY FACT: When an object floats on water, the upward push of the water is equal in size to the downward pull of the Earth.

Getting moving

An **unbalanced** force is needed to:
- start or stop movement
- speed up or slow down.

air
resistance

driving
force

Two forces are shown on the diagram of the cyclist:
- the force to the right is the **driving** force that pushes the cycle along
- the force to the left is the **air resistance** that acts against the movement of the cyclist.

Air resistance is called a resistive force. The faster the cyclist goes the bigger this resistive force gets.

Riding a bicycle

Driving and resistive forces are both at work on a moving cyclist.
- For the cyclist to speed up, the driving force needs to be bigger than the resistive force.
- If the resistive force is bigger than the driving force, the cyclist slows down.
- The only forces acting when the cyclist brakes are resistive forces.

When the cyclist starts to pedal:
- the resistive force is small at first so you speed up quite rapidly
- as your speed increases so does the resistive force
- eventually you get to a speed where the resistive force is equal in size to the driving force
- when this happens you stop speeding up and travel at a constant speed.

The forces acting on an object moving in a straight line at a constant speed are **balanced**. They are the same size but act in opposite directions. Their combined effect is just as if there were no force acting at all.

 KEY FACT: The forces on an object are balanced when it is not moving or not changing its speed or direction.

Resistive forces

Resistive forces are important.

Without resistive forces we cannot walk, and bikes, cars, buses and trains cannot move.

Friction is a resistive force that acts against sliding or slipping.
- If you push an object, friction is the force that slows it down and stops it.
- Friction always acts in the opposite direction to any sliding motion.
- Rough surfaces cause bigger friction forces than smooth ones do.

Ice is a good surface to slide on but a very poor surface to walk or ride a bike on.

How do resistive forces affect movement?

When we walk we rely on friction to stop our feet from slipping.
- To walk forwards our feet push backwards on the ground.
- The friction force stops them from moving backwards and pushes us forward.
- Without friction, our feet would just slip and we would not get anywhere!

Trains also need friction between the wheels and the rails. When wet leaves get on the track the friction force is reduced and the train wheels slip.

Parachutists depend on resistive forces to slow them down. A sky-diver who jumps from an aircraft speeds up to a speed of about 60 m/s. At this speed the air resistance balances the Earth's pull on the sky-diver. Opening the parachute causes the air resistance to get bigger, so the forces acting on the sky-diver are no longer balanced. The sky-diver now slows down.

Eventually the sky-diver falls at a much lower steady speed with the Earth's pull and the air resistance once again in balance.

? ? ? ? Questions ? ? ? ?

1. Why can you run faster than you can swim?
2. A crane lifts a large container. Describe two forces acting on the container. Which force is larger?
3. A man has a mass of 90 kg. What is his weight?
4. A cyclist starts a ride. There are two forces acting on the cyclist – a driving force and a resistive force.
   a. Are the forces balanced or unbalanced at the start? Explain your answer.
   b. What happens to the size of the resistive force as the cyclist increases speed?
   c. Are the forces balanced when the cyclist is travelling at a constant speed? Explain your answer.
   d. Are the forces balanced when the cyclist is braking? Explain your answer.
5. Why is it difficult to walk on ice?
6. Explain why a metal ball sinks but a wooden one of the same size floats.
7. A sky-diver jumps out of an aeroplane. She 'freefalls' for some time and then opens her parachute. Describe how her motion changes. Use ideas of sizes of different forces in your answer.
8. A motor car manufacturer wants to produce a car which uses less petrol. Suggest what could be done to achieve this.

13. The Earth and Beyond

The Solar System

At the centre of the **solar system** is the **Sun**.
The Sun is the solar system's **star**.
It is the source of its light.
Planets are only visible by the sunlight that they **reflect** and so only the half of each planet facing the Sun would be lit up.

Planets Orbit the Sun

The inner planets

There are four planets close to the Sun:
- nearest to the Sun is the tiny planet **Mercury**
- next comes orange **Venus**
- the third planet out is the blue planet **Earth**
- the fourth planet out from the Sun is **Mars.**

The Earth has a satellite of its own, a moon. The Earth's moon takes about twenty eight days to complete an orbit of the Earth. It takes the same time to spin once on its axis, so the same side of the Moon always faces towards the Earth.

Beyond the inner planets

Moving further from the Sun there are a lot of rocky fragments orbiting the Sun between Mars and the first of the outer planets, Jupiter. These fragments of rock, up to 100 km in diameter, form the **asteroid belt**.

The outer planets, in order from the Sun, are:
- **Jupiter,** the largest planet in the Solar System. It has a swirling atmosphere and sixteen moons.
- **Saturn**, the sixth planet, is a very bright yellow object in the sky. It has many rings around it.
- **Uranus** has rings and a total of fifteen satellites, five of which are large moons.
- **Neptune,** the eighth planet, is very similar in size and composition to Uranus.

Planetary motion

The planets
- all go round the Sun in the same direction
- mostly have circular orbits
- move with different speeds. The speed of a planet depends on its distance from the Sun.

Mercury moves fastest of all and it also has the shortest distance to travel to complete an orbit.

The moving Earth

The Sun appears to move across the sky – rising in the east and setting in the west. This apparent movement of the Sun is actually due to the Earth turning round once each day.

The Earth **spins** on its **axis**. This is an imaginary line going through the centre of the Earth from pole to pole. The Earth makes one complete rotation on its axis in one day. This daily rotation of the Earth causes day and night

The number of hours of **daylight** and **darkness** varies throughout the year. This is due to the Earth being **tilted**. When it is summer in Britain the **northern hemisphere** is tilted towards the Sun, so we spend more than twelve hours in daylight. In summer, energy from the Sun is spread over a smaller area than in winter, giving us a warmer climate.

Moving stars

The Earth's spin on its axis makes the stars in the northern sky appear to revolve anticlockwise around the Pole Star, making one complete revolution each twenty-four hours. Stars in the southern sky appear to move round clockwise.

If the Earth's only movement was spinning on its axis, we would see the stars in the same place at the same time each night. But we have to take into account the movement around the Sun:
- as we revolve once around the Sun it looks as if the stars are turning once around the Pole Star
- since there are 365 days in a year and 360° in a circle, the pattern of the stars seems to move by about 1° each day
- if you look at the stars at the same time of night, in one month they should have moved round in the sky by about 30°.

? ? ? ? Questions ? ? ? ?

1. a Which planet orbits the Sun in about 365 days?
   b. Which is the largest planet?
   c. Which planet is nearest to the Sun?
   d. Which two planets have rings round them?

2. Most planets have a circular orbit. Which planet has an elliptical orbit?

3. Mercury takes the shortest time to orbit the Sun. Write down two reasons why Mercury takes the shortest time.

4. This table gives some information about the planets.

Planet	Diameter Earth = 1	Mass Earth = 1	Surface gravitational pull Earth = 1	Density (g/cm³)	Average distance from Sun Earth = 1	Period of orbit (years)
Earth	1	1	1	5.5	1	1
Jupiter	11.2	318	2.6	1.3	5.2	11.9
Mars	0.5	0.1	0.4	4.0	1.5	1.9
Mercury	0.4	0.06	0.4	5.4	0.4	0.2
Neptune	3.8	17	1.2	2.3	30	165
Saturn	9.5	95	1.1	0.7	9.5	29.5
Uranus	3.9	15	0.9	1.6	19	84
Venus	0.95	0.8	0.9	5.2	0.7	0.6

a. What do the inner planets have in common in terms of density?
b. On which planet will 1kg have the greatest weight?
   Explain your choice.
c. Space probes are sent to Jupiter and Mars. Why would it be more difficult to re-launch the probe from Jupiter than Mars?
d. Suggest why Venus appears brighter than Mars when viewed from the Earth.
e. Which planet's orbit is between that of Saturn and Neptune?
f. Which objects orbit the Sun between the inner planets and the outer planets?

5. What is the cause of the apparent movement of the Sun across the sky?
6. What causes the number of hours of daylight to vary during the different seasons?
7. When it is summer in the northern hemisphere, it is winter in the southern hemisphere. Explain why.
8. Why is it warmer in summer than in winter?
9. How many complete revolutions do the stars appear to make around the Pole Star in a non-leap year? Explain your answer.
10. What is the shortest time that it takes for the stars in the group called the Plough to appear to rotate around the Pole Star by 180°? Explain why this could only be observed in winter.

14. Feeding and Digestion

Diet is everything you eat. There are benefits to health in eating a balanced diet.
A balanced diet provides:
* everything required for growth of the body
* everything required for repair of the body
* enough energy for the body's activities.

The human diet should contain **proteins, carbohydrates, fats, vitamins, minerals, fibre** and **water**.

This table gives information about these different food chemicals.

Food chemical	Benefit to the body	Source
proteins	provide amino acids for building and repairing the body. The body cannot store amino acids or proteins	meat, fish, milk, cheese, nuts
carbohydrates (including sugar and starch)	provide energy	bread, potatoes
fats	store energy	butter, oil and margarine
vitamins	required in small quantities to control vital processes in the body	fruit, vegetables contain vitamin C
minerals	required in small amounts for good health, e.g. iron, calcium, iodine	fruit, green vegetables

In addition to the food chemicals, the diet should contain **water** and **dietary fibre** (roughage).
* **Water** acts as a solvent, transports substances and provides a medium where reactions can take place.
* **Fibre** is not digested, but helps in the production of faeces and prevents constipation. There is also evidence that fibre in the diet helps to retain water in the gut cavity and reduces the risk of bowel cancer.

Testing for proteins, carbohydrates and fats in the laboratory

Testing for proteins

The **biuret** test is used to test for proteins.
The food is added to water. Then sodium hydroxide solution and copper (II) sulphate solution are added. A mauve colour shows the presence of protein.

Testing for carbohydrates

There are two tests here – for starch and for simple sugars, such as glucose.
If iodine solution is added to a food containing **starch**, the solution goes dark blue-black.
If Benedict's solution is added to a food containing a **simple sugar** and the mixture is heated, a red-brown solid is formed.

Testing for fats

Ethanol is added to the food being tested in a test tube. The test tube is shaken. The clear liquid is poured into distilled water. If the solution goes milky, a fat is present.
This happens because fat dissolves in ethanol but not in water.

Digestion

Digestion is the breaking down of large insoluble food molecules into small molecules that the body can then absorb and use.

This takes place in the **digestive system**. This is basically one long tube, called the **gut**, several metres long starting at the mouth and finishing at the anus. At different places along the journey food is treated in different ways to break it down and absorb it.

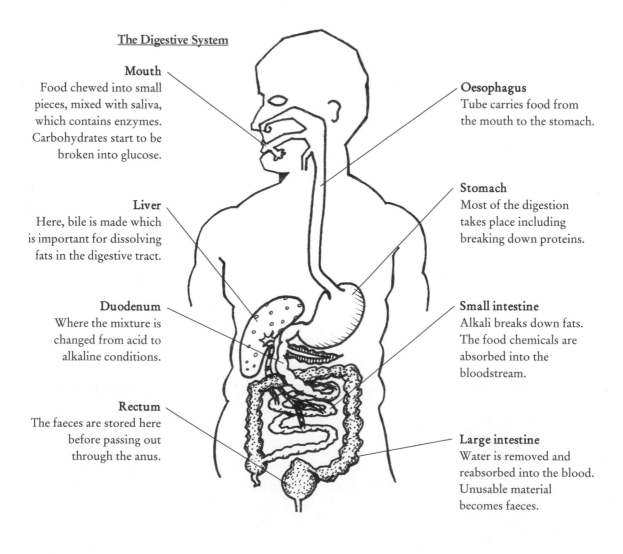

The Digestive System

Mouth
Food chewed into small pieces, mixed with saliva, which contains enzymes. Carbohydrates start to be broken into glucose.

Liver
Here, bile is made which is important for dissolving fats in the digestive tract.

Duodenum
Where the mixture is changed from acid to alkaline conditions.

Rectum
The faeces are stored here before passing out through the anus.

Oesophagus
Tube carries food from the mouth to the stomach.

Stomach
Most of the digestion takes place including breaking down proteins.

Small intestine
Alkali breaks down fats. The food chemicals are absorbed into the bloodstream.

Large intestine
Water is removed and reabsorbed into the blood. Unusable material becomes faeces.

How does food pass along the gut?

Muscles of the gut contract and relax in a special way to squeeze food along the gut. This is called **peristalsis.**

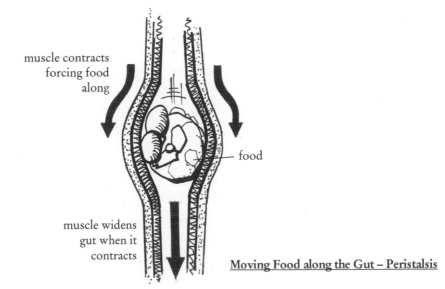

muscle contracts forcing food along

food

muscle widens gut when it contracts

Moving Food along the Gut – Peristalsis

Absorption

Absorption takes place in the small intestine. The food chemicals are absorbed into the bloodstream. The surface of this part of the small intestine, called the **ileum**, is folded with each square millimetre of the surface carrying a large number of finger-like projections called **villi**.

This produces a very large surface area which is very efficient for absorption.
The diagram below shows the cross section of a single villus.

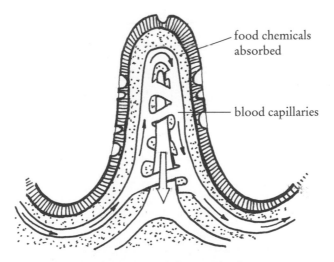

food chemicals absorbed

blood capillaries

Absorbing Food Chemicals into Bloodstream

The wall is very thin and is permeable to the small molecules such as glucose, amino acids, fatty acids and glycerol can pass through the wall into the blood capillaries. Blood from the capillaries joins the rest of the bloodstream.

? ? ? ? Questions ? ? ? ?

1. Why do plants not need a digestive system like animals?
2. Complete the table below by using words from the list

   amino acid   fatty acid   glucose   glycerol

Large food molecule	Small molecule produced
carbohydrate	
protein	
fat	_____ and _____

3. This is a list of some parts of the digestive system.

   anus   duodenum   oesophagus   large intestine   mouth   rectum   small intestine   stomach

   Put these organs in the correct order starting with the mouth and finishing with the anus.

4. Why does the design of the ileum lead to good absorption?

5. Write down three materials absorbed into the bloodstream in the ileum.

6. Why is it important to have a regular supply of protein foods?

7. Why does a marathon runner eat a pasta meal rich in carbohydrates the night before running?

8. If you chew a piece of bread (carbohydrate) for a long time you will notice a sweet taste. Suggest why this is so.

9. The table below gives the results of food tests on three foods, A, B and C.
   Food A is a carbohydrate, B is a protein and C is a fat.
   Finish the table.

Test	A	B	C
protein test			
starch test			
simple sugar test			
fat test			

15. Respiration

Respiration in human cells

Respiration is the process that takes place in all cells to produce energy.
Glucose and **oxygen** reach the cells in the blood supply. In the cells they are converted into **carbon dioxide, water** and **energy.**
Carbon dioxide is transported away from the cells in the blood plasma.

The **word equation** for respiration is:

glucose + oxygen → carbon dioxide + water + energy

The energy released has many uses in the human body.
These include:
1. Movement involved in muscular contractions.
2. Impulses in the nervous system.
3. Releasing heat to maintain a constant body temperature.

Respiration is a process that can be compared to burning.

This table compares the processes of respiration in cells with burning a carbon compound as fuel.

Respiration in cells	Burning a carbon compound as fuel
uses food containing carbon, e.g. glucose	uses fuel containing carbon
uses oxygen	uses oxygen
produces carbon dioxide and water as waste	produces carbon dioxide and water as waste
releases energy, some as heat, some locked up	releases energy, most as heat, some as light

Respiration in plants

Respiration also takes place in plants.
The apparatus in the diagram below shows how carbon dioxide and water are produced by respiration.

A Respiration Experiment

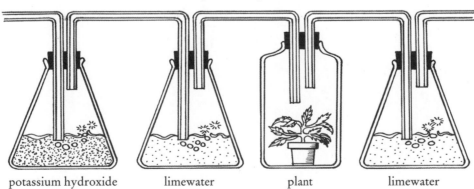

potassium hydroxide   limewater   plant   limewater
solution

Air is drawn through the apparatus by the pump.

Potassium hydroxide solution removes any carbon dioxide in the air.

The first flask of limewater should remain unchanged throughout.

The air then passes through the large jar containing the plant.

The limewater in the second flask should turn milky during the experiment showing that carbon dioxide was formed by the plant.

At the end of the experiment there are droplets of colourless liquid on the inside of the large jar. If this is tested with cobalt chloride paper this paper turns from blue to pink showing water was formed by respiration.

 KEY FACT: Don't forget that respiration also takes place in plants.

? ? ? ? Questions ? ? ? ?

1. a. Describe how respiration in cells in the human body and the combustion of glucose are similar.

   b. Describe any difference between the two processes.

2. Complete the word equation for respiration.
   glucose + _____ → _____ + _____

3. a. What is the reason for using the first flask of limewater?

   b. What would have happened if there was no plant in the flask?

   c. What would happen if a small animal was put in the flask instead of the plant?

16. Breathing in and out

The lungs

This diagram shows the human respiratory system.

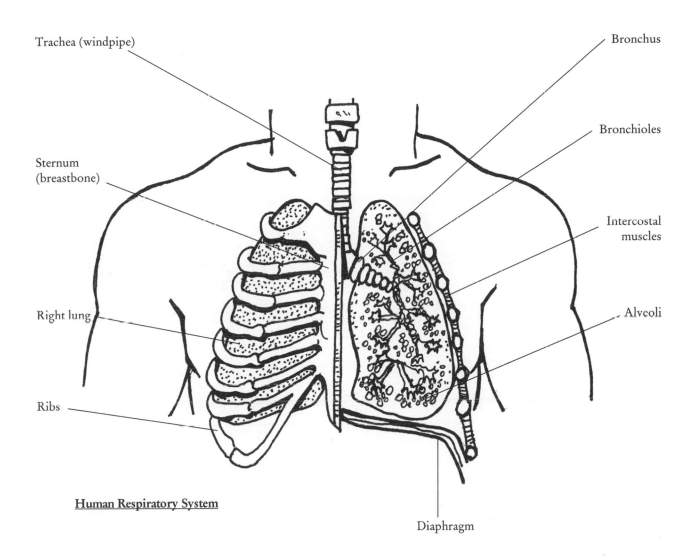

Trachea (windpipe)

Sternum (breastbone)

Right lung

Ribs

Bronchus

Bronchioles

Intercostal muscles

Alvcoli

Diaphragm

<u>Human Respiratory System</u>

The lungs provide a way of getting oxygen into the bloodstream and removing the waste carbon dioxide from the bloodstream. The process is called **gaseous exchange**.

Air is drawn into the lungs by the process of **breathing**.
This is a mechanical process of **inhaling** (breathing in) and **exhaling** (breathing out) air.

When you breathe in:
- the rib cage moves upwards and outwards
- the diaphragm moves downwards
- there is now more space inside your chest (called the **thorax**)
- there is less pressure inside the thorax
- this causes air to be sucked into your lungs.

Gaseous exchange in the lungs

The lung tissue consists of millions of tiny air sacs (called **alveoli**) and blood vessels.
This brings the air and blood in close contact so exchange can take place.
The gaseous exchange takes place efficiently because
- each alveolus has very thin walls so oxygen and carbon dioxide can diffuse through the wall
- the surface of each alveolus is moist
- there is a good blood supply through the blood vessels
- the alveoli have a very large surface area. The total surface of all the alveoli in a human being is about the area of a tennis court.

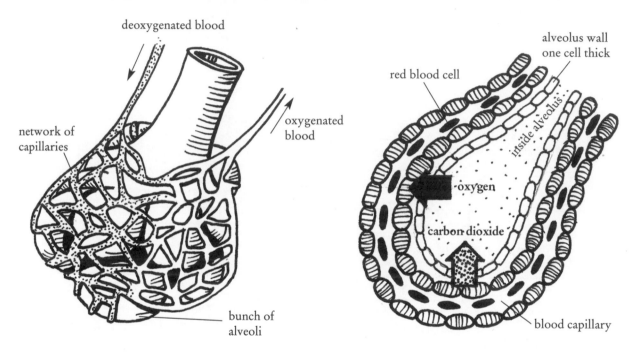

Differences between the air we breathe in and breathe out

The air we breathe out (called exhaled air) is different in composition from the air we breathe in (called inhaled air).

This table gives the typical composition of inhaled and exhaled air.

	Inhaled air	Exhaled air
oxygen	21%	17%
carbon dioxide	0.04%	4%
nitrogen	79%	79%

Notice that we do not use up all the oxygen in the air when we breathe in and breathe out air.

? ? ? ? Questions ? ? ? ?

1. Describe the differences in composition given in the table between inhaled and exhaled air.

2. Describe two other differences between inhaled and exhaled air.

3. A person in hospital is having breathing difficulties. Doctors think breathing would be better if more oxygen was in the lungs.
   a. Why is it important to get oxygen into the lungs?

   b. Suggest what can be done to improve breathing.

   c. Suggest other situations where this might be done.

4. Describe what happens when you breathe out.

17. Microbes and Disease

We know that disease is caused by **micro-organisms** such as **bacteria**, **viruses** and **fungi**.
People sometimes call these germs but this is not a scientific term.
These harmful micro-organisms are too small to be seen. They have to get into the body.

This table summarises some of the similarities and some of the differences between a bacterium and a virus.

Bacterium	Virus
cell wall and cell membrane	protein coat
has genes but no nucleus	has genes
has cytoplasm	no cytoplasm
can reproduce outside living cells	can only reproduce inside living cells
destroyed by antibiotics	not destroyed by antibiotics
bacteria produce toxins (poisons)	viruses damage the cells in which they reproduce

Bacteria multiply very quickly by repeatedly dividing into two.
Viruses cannot reproduce themselves. They can only reproduce inside other cells. This is summarised in the diagram below.

<u>How a Virus Reproduces</u>

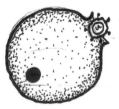

virus attacks cell

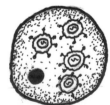

new viruses made inside cell

new viruses escape from cell to infect other cells

How the body prevents micro-organisms entering

- The skin acts as a barrier.
- The breathing organs produce sticky mucus to trap microbes.
- Blood platelets produce clots to seal cuts.

Microbes and Disease

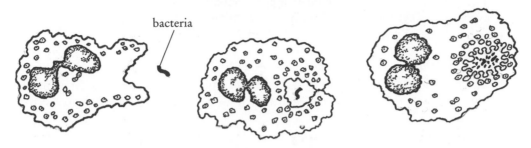

How Antibodies can Destroy Bacteria

bacteria

White blood cells have a defensive role.
1. They engulf and destroy microbes.
2. They produce antibodies that destroy microbes.
3. They produce antitoxins that counteract the toxins produced by microbes.

Once we have had a particular disease, the body knows how to produce **antibodies** and so the white blood cells can produce them quickly before the disease takes hold.
We are said to be **immune** to that microbe.

Sir Alexander Fleming discovered the first antibiotic, called penicillin, by accident.
He noticed in 1928 that staphylococcus (a bacteria) disappeared when in contact with a mould. He concluded that there was an antibacterial substance in the mould.

Penicillin was not developed into a form that could be used until 15 years later.
This was done by HW Florrey and EB Chain.
The ease with which penicillin can be destroyed is one reason why it was difficult to make.
Since then the use of penicillin and other antibiotics has saved millions of lives.

Vaccinations

The idea of preventing people from developing illnesses by injecting a weakened form of the microbe is called vaccination. The white blood cells of the person vaccinated produce antibodies to fight disease.
This can provide protection for diseases such as anthrax, rabies and measles.

? ? ? ? Questions ? ? ? ?

1. Which two features are in a bacterial cell and a human cell?
2. Which two features are not in a virus nor a human cell?
3. Some bacteria get into your body. Initially there are 50 bacteria and they double their number in 20 minutes. How long will it take for there to be 1600 bacteria?
4. You catch a disease caused by bacteria. Why are you unlikely to catch the same disease in the future?
5. SARS is a disease spread by a virus transferred from one person to another by sneezing.
   a. Why is there no antibiotic that can cure this illness?
   b. Suggest ways of preventing this disease transferring from one person to another.

18. Elements

All substances are made up of basic building materials called **elements**.
Sometimes a material is a single element, such as gold or sulphur.
Sometimes it is made up from two or more elements.
These elements may be mixed or combined together.

Elements themselves are made up of tiny particles called **atoms**.
A piece of iron is made up of iron atoms and a piece of sulphur is made of sulphur atoms.
Scientists use shorthand to represent the elements. Each element is given a **symbol**.

Putting elements into groups

Elements can also be grouped as **solids, liquids** and **gases**.
Room temperature is normally 20°C.
An element with a melting point below 20°C is solid at room temperature.
An element with a boiling point below 20°C is gas at room temperature.
An element with a melting point below 20°C and a boiling point above 20°C is a liquid at room temperature.

Chlorine has a melting point of -101°C and a boiling point of -35°C. This means that it is a gas at room temperature because its boiling point is below 20°C.

The Periodic Table

The Periodic Table is a chart showing the names and symbols of all the elements.
The bold line going down through it divides metals on the left-hand side from non-metals on the right-hand side.

Elements

? ? ? ? Questions ? ? ? ?

1. What are the names of the elements with the following symbols?
   a. C _____ ;   b. P _____ ;
   c. Mg _____ ;   d. Cl _____ ;
   e. Zn _____ ;   f. K _____ ;
   g. Hg _____ ;   h. Pb _____ ;
   i. Fe _____ ;   j. Mn_____ .

2. Look at the position of each element in the Periodic Table. Is it a metal or a non-metal?
   a. Chromium_____ ;   b. Selenium _____ ;
   c. Boron _____ ;   d. Fluorine _____ ;
   e. Barium _____ ;   f. Arsenic _____

3. Look at your answers to question 2. Is it true that only metals have names ending in -ium?

19. Mixtures and Compounds

Pure substances

A pure substance is a single substance. It can be an element or a compound.
It contains no **impurities**.
A pure substance melts at a **fixed temperature**.
A mixture melts at a lower temperature than the substances in the mixture and over a range of temperature.

Many everyday substances are **mixtures**.

Mixture	Composition
air	80% nitrogen and 20% oxygen with small quantities of other gases
sea water	water with large range of dissolved solids including sodium chloride
petroleum	mixture of different compounds of carbon and hydrogen
metal alloy e.g. brass	a mixture of metals – brass is copper and zinc

Differences between pure substances and mixtures

This table gives the differences between a pure substance (element or compound) and a mixture.

Pure substance	Mixture
contains a single element or elements joined in fixed proportions	contains elements or compounds in proportions that are not fixed
difficult or impossible to separate elements in a compound	elements can be separated
properties of a compound are different from the elements combined together	properties of the mixture are the same as the properties of the things making it up
energy is often given out when a compound is formed	no energy change when a mixture is formed
melts and boils at a fixed temperature	melts at a lower temperature than the pure substance and over a range of temperatures; boils at a higher temperature than the pure substance

Compound formation

Under certain conditions, some mixtures of elements can **combine** together to form a **compound**.

Mixtures and Compounds

Hydrogen and oxygen

A mixture of hydrogen and oxygen is a colourless gas. When a lighted splint is put into a mixture of hydrogen and oxygen an explosion takes place. Hydrogen and oxygen atoms join together to form liquid water. Two hydrogen atoms combine with one atom of oxygen to form one **molecule** of water.

A chemical reaction where elements combine to form a compound is called **synthesis**. The reaction can be represented by a word equation:

      Hydrogen + oxygen → water

Iron and sulphur

A mixture of iron and sulphur combine when heated to form a compound called **iron (II) sulphide.** This can be summarised by a diagram.

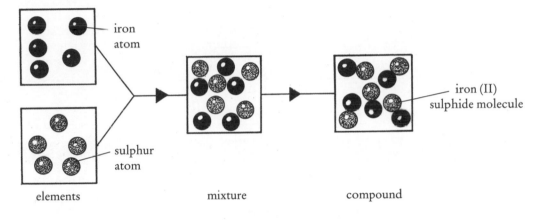

iron atom

sulphur atom

iron (II) sulphide molecule

elements   mixture   compound

The mixture of iron and sulphur can be separated using a magnet.
Iron and sulphur cannot be separated from the compound iron sulphide.
When the reaction takes place one **atom** of iron joins with one **atom** of sulphur to form one **molecule** of iron (II) sulphide.
This can be summarised by a word equation:

      Iron + sulphur → iron (II) sulphide

Naming compounds

Where a compound is composed of two elements the name ends in **-ide**.
If there is a metal in the compound, the metal is named first. E.g. magnesium oxide is a compound of magnesium and oxygen.

Where a compound contains more than two elements and one of the elements is oxygen the compound ends in **-ate**. Sodium sulphate is a compound of sodium, sulphur and oxygen.

Properties of compounds

The properties of a compound are different from the elements that make it up.
A mixture of the elements hydrogen and oxygen is a gas but the compound water is a liquid.

In the same way that each element has a symbol, each compound has a **formula**.
The **formula** of iron (II) sulphide is written as FeS. This shows that one atom of iron combines with one atom of sulphur.

Mixtures and Compounds

This table gives the names and formulae of some common compounds. It also gives the numbers of atoms of the different elements present in the formula.

Name	Formula	Number of atoms of different elements present
sodium chloride	$NaCl$	1 atom of sodium and 1 atom of chlorine
calcium chloride	$CaCl_2$	1 atom of calcium and 2 atoms of chlorine
zinc oxide	ZnO	1 atom of zinc and 1 atom of oxygen
calcium carbonate	$CaCO_3$	1 atom of calcium, 1 atom of carbon and three atoms of oxygen
copper sulphate	$CuSO_4$	1 atom of copper, 1 atom of sulphur and 4 oxygen atoms
sodium nitrate	$NaNO_3$	1 sodium atom, 1 atom of nitrogen and 3 atoms of oxygen

? ? ? ? Questions ? ? ? ?

1. Nitrogen and hydrogen combine to form nitrogen hydride (often called ammonia).
   In ammonia one nitrogen atom is combined with three hydrogen atoms.
   Write a word equation for the reaction.
2. A certain acid has a melting point of 76°C.
   A sample of this acid melts between 70 – 73°C.
   What does this suggest about this sample?
3. Potassium chlorate is a compound of three elements.
   a. What are these three elements?
   b. When potassium chlorate is heated, potassium chloride is formed.
      What is the other product?
   c. Write a word equation for the reaction that has taken place.
4. The composition of air varies from place to place but the composition of water is fixed.
   What does this tell you about air and water?
5. Here is a list of copper compounds.
   copper (II) oxide
   copper (II) hydroxide
   copper (II) chloride
   copper (II) sulphate
   copper (II) nitrate
   a. Which of these compounds does not contain oxygen?
   b. Which compounds contain two elements?
   c. Which compounds contain three elements?
   d. Copper (II) nitrate decomposes when heated to produce copper(II) oxide.
      The other products are nitrogen dioxide and oxygen gases.
      i. Which product is an element?
      ii. Write a word equation for this reaction.

60

20. Rocks

A rock is a solid part of the Earth's crust. Some rocks are almost pure substances but most are mixtures of chemicals called **minerals**.

The properties of a rock will depend upon:

- the type of minerals
- the concentration of minerals in the rock
- how the minerals are held together.

Rocks can be classified as **sedimentary rocks**, **metamorphic rocks** and **igneous rocks**.

Sedimentary rocks

When existing rocks are broken down by **weathering** small bits are broken off. These bits are washed along in rivers. When the speed of water slows, the bits settle as **sediment**. These sediments are then compressed by other rocks and the grains cemented together. This process can take millions of years.

New rocks are deposited on existing rocks and so the older rocks are the lower they are in the Earth's crust.

the lower the layer, the older the rock

Sedimentary Rock Layers

This diagram shows layers of rock. After they are formed these layers can tilt and fold.

Sedimentary rocks are not crystalline but are made up of grains. Sedimentary rocks may contain fossils.

The table gives examples of sedimentary rocks.

Rock	What it is made of
sandstone	grains of sand cemented together
shale or mudstone	like sandstone but made of smaller paarticles
limestone	shells of millions of marine animals cemented together
conglomerate	large pebbles cemented together

Metamorphic rocks

High temperatures and high pressures turn sedimentary rocks into metamorphic rocks. These rocks may be non-crystalline or contain tiny crystals.

Both limestone and marble are made of the same chemical. They are both calcium carbonate in the form of calcite. Limestone (sedimentary rock) is made of tiny **grains** and **marble** (metamorphic rocks) is made of **crystals**. The change takes place when the rock is heated to a high temperature or compressed to a high pressure or both.

Another metamorphic rock is **slate**. This is made when the sedimentary rock called **mudstone** is compressed to a high pressure.

Fossils are found in sedimentary rocks and sometimes in metamorphic rocks. Where they exist in metamorphic rocks they are often distorted.

Igneous rocks

Igneous rocks are formed when the hot magma inside the Earth is cooled and crystallises. The size of the crystals depends on the rate of cooling.

rapid cooling – small crystals   slow cooling – large crystals

This table compares two igneous rocks – granite and basalt.

Granite	Basalt
usually pink or grey in colour	usually dark grey but can be black, brown or green in colour
large crystals	small crystals

Weathering

Weathering is the process which breaks down exposed rocks by the action of rain, frost, wind and other elements of weather.

Weathering can take place in two main ways:

1. Mechanical weathering
This is sometimes called physical weathering.
During the day rocks heat up and expand. At night they cool and this cooling causes stresses within the rock. When this happens over and over again it breaks down the rock.

If there are cracks in the rock, water gets into the cracks. When water freezes, ice forms and expands. This breaks down the rocks.
This is sometimes called 'freeze-thaw'.

Freeze-thaw Method of Mechanical Weathering

water enters crack in rock

ice

on freezing ice expands causing
the rock to crack open

2. Chemical weathering

This is the breaking down of rocks by chemical reactions.
Calcium carbonate (limestone) is broken down by rain water.
Rain water contains dissolved carbon dioxide. This forms carbonic acid.
Carbonic acid attacks the limestone forming calcium hydrogencarbonate. This dissolves
in water.

Rock cycle

In a similar way to the way bottles are recycled, inside the Earth existing rocks can be taken
back into the magma and new rocks formed. This is summarised in the diagram below.

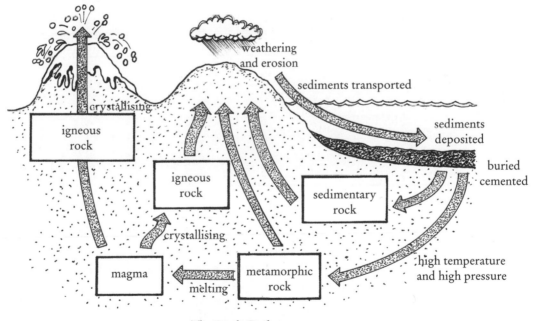

The Rock Cycle

Rocks are being broken down and new rocks are being formed all the time.
When the magma crystallises, **igneous** rocks are formed.
These are broken down by **weathering** and **erosion** to form sediments.
Sediments are deposited and converted into **sedimentary** rocks.
At high temperatures and pressures sedimentary rocks can be changed into **metamorphic**
rocks. Rocks returning to the magma complete the cycle.

The rock cycle is driven by two energy processes:
1. powered by the Sun's energy
2. powered from energy from radioactive decay inside the Earth

? ? ? ? Questions ? ? ? ?

1. Write down the names of two sedimentary rocks, two metamorphic rocks and two igneous rocks.
   Sedimentary
   Metamorphic
   Igneous

2. What evidence is there that granite is crystallised inside the earth while basalt is crystallised on its surface?

3. Rocks are widely used for building.
This table gives information about four commonly used rocks.

Rock	Type of rock	Minerals present	Properties of rock
granite	igneous	feldspar, quartz	very hard, attractive when polished
marble	metamorphic	calcite	hard, attractive appearance, slippery when wet, attacked by acid rain
limestone	sedimentary	calcite	quite hard, attacked by acid rain, relatively cheap
sandstone	sedimentary	quartz	moderately hard but crumbles to form sand, relatively cheap

   a. Which two rocks contain the same minerals?
   b. A plaque is to be placed in the city centre. The plaque is exposed to all weathers. Which rock would you choose? Explain your answer.
   c. A long path is to be built. The path is to be covered with rock chippings. Which rock should be used? Explain your answer.
   d. Why would marble be unsuitable for the surrounds of a swimming pool?

4. Complete the word equation for the chemical weathering of limestone.
   carbon dioxide + water → _____
   calcium carbonate + _____ → _____

21. Moving Energy Around

If you leave the door of a hot oven open, the oven will start to cool down. However, if you leave the door of a cold freezer open, it will start to warm up.
An object that is warmer than its surroundings loses energy.
An object that is cooler gains energy.

There are different ways in which energy can be transferred.

Conduction

A metal poker in a hot fire gets hot all along its length. Energy is transferred along the poker by **conduction**.
In conduction energy is transferred from particle to particle. The particles in contact with the fire have more energy than the particles at the cool end of the poker. The particles at the warm end vibrate more than those at the cool end. Energy is transferred from particle to particle by means of vibrations.

Solids and liquids conduct heat energy better than gases because the particles are closer together and can pass on their energy more readily.

Metals are the best conductors because electrons can move through metals, taking energy with them to all parts of the metal.

Convection

Look, for example, at a mug of coffee. Energy that flows through the walls of the mug is carried away by **convection currents** in the surrounding air.
This happens in three steps.
1. The air near the outside of the walls becomes heated.
2. This air expands and becomes less dense.
3. This warm, less dense air rises and is replaced by cooler air.

 KEY FACT: Convection currents are explained by changes in density caused by heating and cooling. Often students give vague answers in terms of heat rising and cold falling. Heat and cold are not substances.

Evaporation

A lot of energy is lost through the surface of the cup of coffee. If you put a lid over the top the coffee stays hot for much longer.
Energy is lost from the surface of the coffee by **evaporation**.
When a liquid evaporates:
 • the particles with a lot of energy near the surface leave the liquid and vapour
 • this reduces the average energy of the particles remaining in the liquid
 • as a result the liquid loses energy and its temperature falls.

Radiation

All objects emit energy as **electromagnetic radiation**.
Every object radiates energy, but the hotter the object is the more energy it will radiate.
For most objects, this energy is **infra-red radiation**
Very hot objects can also radiate energy as **light** and other forms of electromagnetic radiation.

Heat and temperature

Which is hotter, a bath full of hot water or the filament of an electric light bulb that is giving out light?
The correct answer is the bulb filament.
Its temperature is around 2000°C, whereas the bath's temperature is about 50°C.

Although the bath water is cooler than the bulb filament, it takes more **energy** to heat up the bath water from cold than the filament.

This is because:
- it takes more energy to heat 1 kg of water by each degree Celsius than it does to heat 1 kg of bulb filament
- there is much more water to be heated than bulb filament.

 KEY FACT: The temperature of an object is a measure of its hotness. It does not show the amount of energy needed for the object to become hot.

Insulation

In a modern house the builder includes many materials to prevent energy being lost from the house to the surroundings.
This is called **insulation.**
There is:
- insulation in the loft to reduce energy losses through the roof
- insulation foam in the walls between layers of bricks
- insulation in the floor to reduce energy losses through the floor
- an air gap in double glazed windows to reduce energy losses through windows.

Air is a good insulator. This is because air is very poor at conducting energy in the form. Air is very good at forming convection currents, so to make it an insulator, it needs to be trapped so that it cannot move.

Air is trapped between layers of clothing and pockets of air are trapped in foam insulation. This prevents energy transfer from taking place through convection currents and minimises energy transfer by conduction.

Two other methods of minimising the energy transfer between hot and cold objects are:
- covering a liquid to reduce the energy loss through evaporation. This is very effective in keeping hot drinks hot.
- wrapping an object in aluminium foil to reduce the energy loss through infra-red radiation. Foil reflects radiant energy in the same way that a mirror reflects light.

 KEY FACT: Insulation is used to keep things cool as well as warm.
There is a lot of insulation in an oven and a freezer.

Moving Energy Around

? ? ? ? Questions ? ? ? ?

1. Take away meals are sometimes packed in shiny aluminium containers and sometimes in a foam pack. Explain why these two types of packaging keep the food hot.

2. Why in cold weather do several layers of clothes keep you warmer than one thick layer?

3. Explain why trapped air is a good insulator but air that is free to move is a poor insulator.

4. A modern house has two walls with air in the 'cavity' between them.
Explain how filling the cavity with foam, plastic blocks or mineral wool insulates the house.

5. Explain why outdoor swimming pools are often covered with a polythene sheet at night.

6. Explain what causes convection currents.

22. Magnets and Electromagnets

Magnets

A **magnet**:
- attracts iron, steel, cobalt and nickel
- does not affect materials that are not metals, copper, brass, chrome, magnesium or zinc.

A magnet can sort steel drink cans from aluminium ones.

Iron is easy to **magnetise** (i.e. make it into a magnet) but it quickly loses its magnetism.

Steel is harder to magnetise but, once magnetised, it keeps its magnetism for a long time.
- A magnet that is free to turn round always points with one **pole** towards magnetic north.
- This is called the **north-seeking pole** or north pole of the magnet.
- The opposite pole is called the **south-seeking** or south pole.

Magnets can **attract** and **repel** other magnets. The strongest parts of a magnet are called the **poles**. Bar magnets have poles at the ends.

Opposite poles **attract**.
Similar poles **repel**.

The north-seeking pole of a magnet is attracted to the Earth's north pole, so they must have opposite magnetism.

Magnetic fields

A magnet lines up north-south. A **compass** uses a small magnet pivoted on a needle to enable it to turn round so that the poles point towards magnetic north and south. However, if a compass is placed near a magnetic material such as iron, it will point towards that material instead.
A compass can be used to investigate the **attractive** and **repulsive** forces around a magnet. By looking at the direction of the force on the north-seeking pole of the compass, a set of lines can be drawn showing the force pattern all around the magnet. This is called a **magnetic field pattern**.

<u>Magnetic Field Patterns Around a Bar Magnet</u>

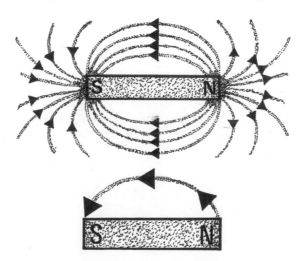

It shows where a magnet pushes and pulls magnetic objects around it.
Magnetic field patterns are always drawn to show the direction of the force on the north-seeking pole of another magnet.

Iron filings act like small compasses. They can be used to show a magnetic field pattern but do not show its direction.

Electromagnets

When an electric current is passing through a wire it produces a magnetic field around it. The diagrams below show the magnetic field around a straight wire and a coil.

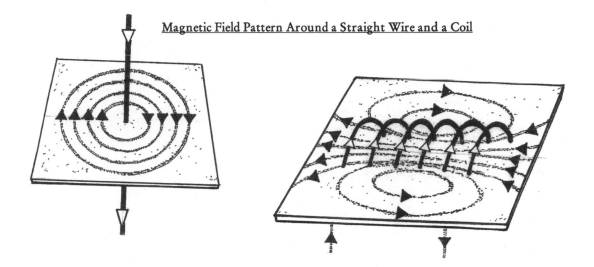

<u>Magnetic Field Pattern Around a Straight Wire and a Coil</u>

Electromagnetic forces can be made much bigger by wrapping a **coil** of wire around an iron **core**.
When a current passes in the wire, the iron becomes strongly magnetised.
Apart from adding an iron core, the strength of an electromagnet can be increased by using a larger current and more turns on the coil.

An electromagnet is useful because:
- it can be switched on and off
- its strength can be varied.

Electromagnets are widely used:
- in electric motors in electric drills, lawnmowers etc
- to make a loudspeaker cone vibrate
- to store information in magnetic form on audio and video tapes and computer disks.

Using electromagnets

A useful electromagnet is made using a coil of wire on an iron core. This can cause movement when the magnet is switched on and off.
Motors, bells and **relays** all use electromagnets.

A **relay** is a switch operated by switching an electromagnet on and off.

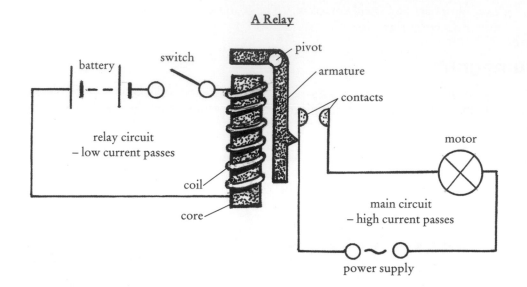

A Relay

When the relay is switched on:
- current passes in the relay coil, creating a magnetic field
- the iron core becomes magnetised
- the armature is attracted to the core
- the switch contacts are pressed together and the light comes on.

A relay:
- can operate from a low voltage source and be used to switch devices that work from a higher voltage
- only needs a small current to operate it.

The electrical circuits in cars carry large currents that need thick wires. Relays are used so that thin wires can be used for the switches that the driver operates.

Magnets and Electromagnets

? ? ? ? Questions ? ? ? ?

1. Which of the following materials are attracted to a magnet? Underline these materials.

   iron   magnesium   plastic   steel   wood

2. Complete the sentences by adding words from the list.

   attract   repel

   When the north poles of two magnets are brought close together they _____.

   When the north pole of one magnet is brought close to the south pole of another they _____.

3. Some coins are made of an alloy of copper and zinc. Others are made of steel coated with copper.

   How could these coins be easily separated by the bank?

4. Explain why steel is better than iron for making permanent magnets.

5. Which end of a compass needle normally points towards the Earth's north pole?

6. Explain why a magnetic compass cannot be used to steer a ship that is made of steel.

7. Describe how the direction of the magnetic field differs on the inside and outside of the coil.

8. An electromagnet is made by winding a coil of wire on a cardboard roll.
   Using steel paper clips describe how an investigation can be carried out to find the effect of increasing current on the strength of an electromagnet.

9. Describe how the relay contacts become pressed together when a current passes in the coil.

10. Some outside lights switch on automatically at dusk. The sensing circuit operates from a low voltage supply. Explain why a relay is used to switch the lamp.

Light travels in straight lines

Light from a torch is shone onto a screen.
When an opaque object (i.e. one that does not let light pass through it) is put between the light source and the screen a sharp **shadow** is formed.
This is because light does not pass through the opaque object.

A shadow provides evidence that light **travels in straight lines**.

During a thunderstorm you see a flash of lightning before you hear the rumble of thunder. This is because of the different speeds of light and sound.

Light travels at one million times faster than the speed of sound in air.

Because of the very fast speed of light, there is normally no noticeable time delay between an event happening and us seeing it.

Exceptions to this occur when the distances are vast, for example when looking at stars. Observations of our Sun see what happened eight and a half minutes ago. Light from the second nearest star to us takes more than four years to get here, so when you are star-gazing you are looking back in time!

Seeing

In order to see, we have to use the eyes and the brain.
- The eyes are the **sensors**. They send electrical signals along the optic nerve to the brain.
- The brain interprets the signals. It assumes that the light travelled to the eyes in a straight line.
- This enables the brain to work out where things are.
- The brain needs messages from both eyes to be able to position an object exactly.

Luminous and non-luminous objects

Objects that are **luminous** give out light themselves.
Other objects that do not give out light will **scatter** light (i.e. reflect it in all directions).
These objects are **non-luminous**.

Mirrors

Mirrors do not reflect light in all directions like most objects.
They reflect it in a **regular** and **predictable** way.
Light is reflected from a mirror at the same angle as it hits it.
A flat mirror can be a piece of glass with a silver coloured reflective surface behind it or a polished flat piece of metal. Such a flat mirror is called a **plane mirror**.
In the diagram on page 73 the light ray is hitting the plane mirror. The line drawn at right angles to a mirror is called the **normal line.**
The angle between the light ray hitting the mirror (called the **incident ray**) and the normal line is equal to the angle between the ray leaving the mirror (called the **reflected ray**) and the normal line.

angle of incidence = angle of reflection

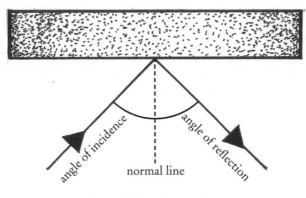

Light Reflected in a Mirror

Imagine you are looking into a plane mirror. This confuses your brain. It starts to see things that aren't really there.

Light from each part of the face hits the mirror and is reflected at equal angles. The reflected light is detected by the eyes. The brain then 'sees' the face, and works out where it is, assuming that the light has travelled in straight lines.

It 'sees' a face behind the mirror.

What you see is called a **virtual image**.

Image means likeness. You see a likeness of your face in the mirror. The image is virtual because, unlike the image that you see on a television or cinema screen, it is not really there.

Finding the image

Using the rule about the way in which light is reflected at a mirror, you can construct images.

If you do this you will see that the image in a plane mirror:
- is always formed straight behind the mirror
- is the same distance behind the mirror as the object is in front of it.

Periscopes are used to see over people in a crowd or by people in submarines who want to see what is above the surface of the sea when the submarine is submerged.

Mirrors can be used in periscopes to turn light round corners.

Light hitting a mirror at an angle of 45° is reflected at the same angle and so is turned through 90°.

Changing the speed of light

Have you ever tried to catch a coin in a pond with your hand? It is not as easy as it seems because the coin does not appear to be as deep in the pond as it really is.

This is another example of your eye-brain system being fooled when light does not travel in straight lines.

When light passes from air into water there is a **change in the speed** at which light travels. This can also cause a **change in direction**.

As light enters water or any other dense transparent material it slows down.

The change in speed of light as it enters water or glass is called **refraction**.

The diagram below shows how, because of refraction of light, the coin does not appear to be as deep as it really is.

The dotted lines in the diagram show where the light appears to have come from, assuming that it has travelled in straight lines. This is another example of a **virtual image**. As with a mirror, the virtual image is just like the original object, except that it is not really there.

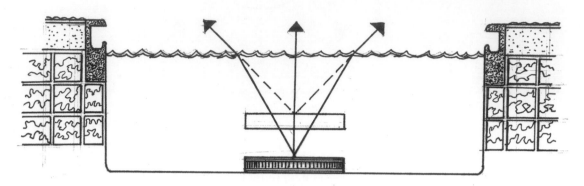

The Coin Appears to be Closer than it is.

The same thing happens when a light ray passes through a block of glass.
The diagrams below show the effect of the change in speed when light passes through a block of glass.

- The light that meets the air-glass boundary at an angle of 90° carries on without a change in direction.
- At any other angle the light changes direction as it goes into and leaves the glass block.

Refraction of Light

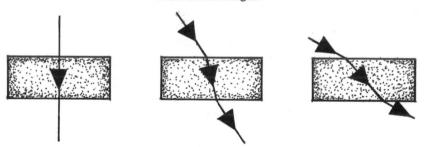

Colour

White light can be separated when it is passed through a triangular block of glass or plastic. This is called **dispersion**.
The colours are:

    red
    orange
    yellow
    green
    blue
    indigo
    violet

These are called the colours of the **spectrum**. This dispersion is caused because the different colours of light travel at different speeds through the prism.

Light

 KEY FACT: You can remember the order of the colours by remembering the name ROY G BIV.

When it is both rainy and sunny, you may see a **rainbow**. This is caused by dispersion of white light in water droplets.

If you mix all of these seven colours together, you will get white light by colour **addition**.

? ? ? ? Questions ? ? ? ?

1. Which of the following are luminous and which are non-luminous?

   Aeroplane   Candle flame   Lit electric light bulb   Moon   Sun

   Luminous

   Non-luminous

2. Which of the following are opaque?

   glass window   metal object   perspex goggles   wooden block

3. Why is the shadow formed when an opaque object is placed between a light source and a screen sharp rather than fuzzy?

4. Explain why you would see the flash from a distant cannon when it is fired before you hear the sound.

5. What is the advantage of having two eyes rather than one?

24. Sound and Hearing

Producing sound

A **sound** is made when something **vibrates** in a to-and-fro motion.

Some musical instruments, e.g. a guitar, have strings that vibrate when they are plucked. Other musical instruments, e.g. a recorder, have columns of air that vibrate when they are blown.

Televisions, radios and hi-fi all use **loudspeakers** to reproduce sound. A loudspeaker consists of a paper cone driven backwards and forwards by an electromagnet.

<u>Loudspeaker</u>

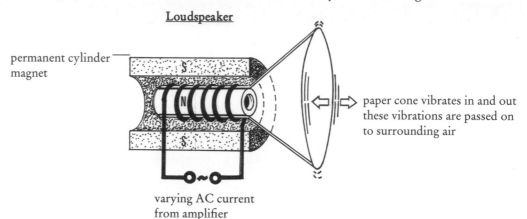

permanent cylinder magnet

paper cone vibrates in and out these vibrations are passed on to surrounding air

varying AC current from amplifier

Travelling sound

Sound travels through anything that has particles to transmit the vibrations. It travels very fast in solids, where the particles are close together, slower in liquids and slowest of all in gases.

Sound cannot travel through a vacuum because there are no particles to transfer vibrations.

Hearing

In an ear:
- sound waves cause vibrations of the **ear drum** in the outer ear
- the **ossicles** are three bones in the middle ear that transfer this energy to the inner ear
- in the inner ear **nerve endings** are stimulated by the vibration and send messages along the auditory nerve to the brain.

outer ear   middle ear   inner ear

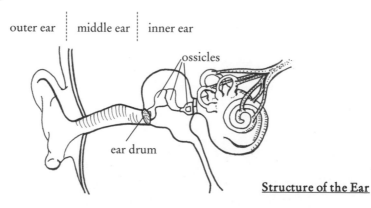

ossicles

ear drum

<u>Structure of the Ear</u>

A normal young person can detect sounds with a frequency ranging from about 20Hz to about 20 000 Hz.

As a person gets older the range of frequencies that can be heard is reduced.
A middle-aged person may not be able to hear sounds with a frequency greater than 15 000 Hz although the hearing at low frequencies is less likely to be affected.

People who work in noisy environments should wear ear muffs to protect their ears from damage. Sudden exposure to a loud sound such as an explosion can cause immediate damage by breaking the ear drum or the ossicles.

Different sounds

As a wave moves along a **slinky spring**, each part of the spring vibrates. The particles in air vibrate in a similar way when they transmit sound. Each wave consists of a **squash**, where the particles are close together, followed by a **stretch**, where the particles are further apart. A hand pushing and pulling a slinky spring is a good model of what happens when a loudspeaker cone is pushing and pulling on the air.

<u>Moving Waves Along a Slinky Spring</u>

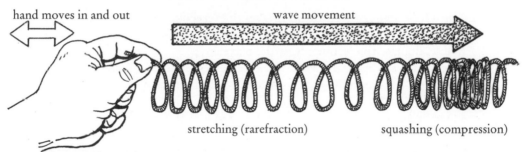

hand moves in and out   wave movement

stretching (rarefraction)   squashing (compression)

- **Moving the hand further** has the same effect on the spring as **turning up the volume control** has on the air particles.
- The particles **move further** and you hear a **louder** sound.
- When you push further you are increasing the **amplitude** of the vibration.

The **amplitude** of the vibration is the greatest distance that each part of the slinky moves from its rest position. A microphone and an oscilloscope can be used to plot a graph that shows the movement of air particles when a sound wave passes. The upwards and downwards movement of the oscilloscope trace represents the forwards and backwards movement of an air particle.

Higher and louder

The trace on an oscilloscope screen shows the number of sound waves that are detected in a certain time. Adjusting the oscilloscope settings can change this time. A "crest" and a "trough" represent one complete wave.

<u>Traces on an Oscilloscope</u>

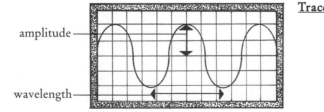

amplitude

wavelength

There are now more waves in the same time; the **frequency** (the number of waves per second) has increased.

Frequency is measured in **hertz (Hz)**.
1 Hz = 1 wave per second.

These measurements using an oscilloscope display show that:
- increasing the **amplitude** of a sound wave makes it sound louder
- increasing the **frequency** of a sound wave gives it a higher pitch.

? ? ? ? Questions ? ? ? ?

1. A sound wave has a frequency of 200 Hz. How many waves of sound pass in 10 s?

2. The oscilloscope trace shown above shows the number of waves of a sound that happen in 1/20 s (0.05 s).

   a. How many waves are shown on the screen?

   b. Calculate the frequency of the wave.

3. Why is a huge explosion in space not heard on Earth?

4. Describe how sound waves are detected by the ear.

5. Describe the relationship between the loudness of a sound and the amplitude of vibration of the air particles.

25. Inheritance and Selection

Passing on information to the next generation

Apart from mature red blood cells, all the cells in the human body contain a **nucleus**.
The nucleus of a cell contains chemical codes called **genes**. These have information to control the action of the cell and to enable new cells to be made.

All the nuclei of body cells (apart from sex cells) of an individual contain identical genes.
Each sex cells contains only half of the genetic information of body cells.
The chances of two sex cells containing identical information are tiny.

The single cell that is the beginning of a new individual is formed at **fertilisation**.
At **fertilisation** a male sex cell (sperm) fuses with a female sex cell (ovum).
The nucleus of the new cell, which is the beginning of a new individual, contains genes inherited from each parent.

These inherited genes will control the development of the individual and determine some of its characteristics, for example eye colour and blood group.

Inheriting information

Brothers and sisters in the same family often share characteristics.
You can often recognise these characteristics but, unless they are identical twins, the chance of two brothers or two sisters having identical genes is virtually zero.

Identical twins have identical genes because they are formed when the developing embryo splits into two cells.

Brothers and sisters have similar characteristics because they have some genes in common.
They have differences because they do not have all genes the same.

 KEY FACT: Sexual reproduction causes variation within individuals.

Variation

The ways in which one individual living thing differs from another is called **variation**.
There are two types of variation.

1. Discontinuous variation
e.g. blood groups. There are four main groups of blood: A, B, AB and O.
A person cannot have two blood groups. They must be in one group or another.

2. Continuous variation
e.g. height or weight. If you look at a group of people you will find a whole range of different heights. All heights are possible.

What causes variation in people?

Individual people inherit different combinations of genes from their parents. There are so many possible combinations that every person is different. Some of the differences between people are due only to the genes that they inherit. These **genetic factors** include:
- eye colour

- natural hair colour
- blood group.

Some differences are due only to **environmental factors** such as diet, climate and lifestyle.
These include:
- whether the ears are pierced or not
- whether they have long hair or short hair
- whether the person is a smoker or a non-smoker.

Most characteristics are affected by both genetic and environmental factors.
An individual's height and weight are both affected by:
- the genes inherited from the parents
- their diet
- how much and what type of exercise they take.

Natural skin colour is determined genetically, but the actual colour of a person's skin is affected by environmental factors such as exposure to the Sun and the use of cosmetics.

Asexual reproduction or cloning

Sexual reproduction produces variation in offspring.
The genes from two parents can combine in many different ways. Each combination produces a different individual.

Some simple animals and some plants can reproduce so that the offspring have identical genes to a single parent.
This is known as **asexual reproduction** or **cloning**.

Cloning plants

A gardener has a single red geranium plant. He can produce many more identical plants.
He cuts small pieces (called cuttings) from the stem of the parent plant and plants these cuttings in compost.
All the cuttings that grow into plants have genes identical to the parent.
So all the characteristics of the young plants are the same, including the colour of their flowers.

Taking Cuttings to Produce New Plants

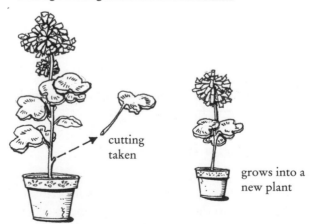

cutting taken

grows into a new plant

This is not a new scientific technique. Plants have been produced in this way for thousands of years.

Some plants reproduce easily from cuttings, and others do not.

More recently techniques have been developed to grow rare plants from just a few cells of the parent plant. These are cultured in a suitable solution, rich in minerals. Thousands of identical plants can be produced from one plant.

Cloning animals

Some animals consist of just one cell. An example is the amoeba. This often lives in ponds. It does not have any organs or sex cells so it cannot reproduce sexually.

As an amoeba grows, the nucleus copies itself and then the cell divides into two, producing two identical individuals from only one.

Reproducing Amoeba

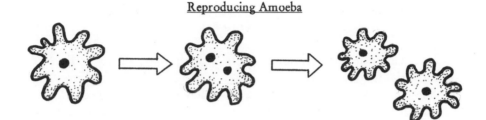

Only simple animals can clone themselves like this. Some female aphids can reproduce thousands of offspring asexually. This has the advantage that reproduction is very rapid, but there are also disadvantages.

There is no variation in the offspring.

This is why most aphids, such as greenfly, reproduce sexually.

In recent years complex animals have been artificially cloned. Dolly the sheep was cloned by scientists in a laboratory. She was an exact copy of her mother. Her life was, however, shorter than might have been expected. Scientists have also cloned horses and other mammals. At some stage it might be possible to clone people.

Many people think that cloning is morally wrong.

Others think it could benefit people if animals could be cloned.

Selective breeding of animals

Dairy farmers want to improve the quality of their herd so that the cows give more milk. They do this by **selective breeding**.

To increase the cows' milk yields by selective breeding, farmers:
- choose the cows with the highest milk yields to breed from
- from the offspring, choose those with the highest milk yields to breed the next generation.

They repeat this over several generations, which gradually improves the milk yields.

Selective breeding of plants

New varieties of plant with the desired characteristics can be produced by **selective breeding**. This involves **cross-pollination**.

- Pollen from the flowers of plants with some of the desired characteristics is gathered.
- This is then used to pollinate the flowers of plants with other desirable characteristics.

For this to be successful, plant breeders have to make sure that the flowers being pollinated have not already been pollinated by pollen from flowers of the same type. They also need the flowers that provide the pollen to be ready at the same time as those that are to receive it.

? ? ? ? Questions ? ? ? ?

1. a. Describe what happens at fertilisation.
   b. How do the number of genes present in cells change during fertilisation?

2. Sam has some pink geranium plants. They have become spindly. She wants to produce new plants for next year.
   She could take cuttings or could grow new plants from seeds. What are the advantages and disadvantages of these two methods of producing new plants?

3. Place a tick or ticks in the columns of the table below to show whether each characteristic shown on the left is genetic, environmental or a combination of both.

Characteristic	Genetic	Environmental
natural colour of finger nails		
colour of eyes		
length of finger nails		
length of feet		
length of hair		

4. Different varieties of tomatoes are available. Some suit a gardener growing tomatoes at home. Others suit the commercial grower who is growing tomatoes for sale in supermarkets.
   What characteristics would each type of grower be looking for?

'Children are fatter and less fit than previous generations.'

You may have read reports in newspapers about people becoming more overweight and less fit than previous generations. People eat more and have diets rich in fats. They use cars more and so take less exercise.

There are two aspects of fitness:
1. The ability to perform certain physical tasks.
2. The speed of recovery after the activity.

Look back at the section on breathing and respiration (page 49).

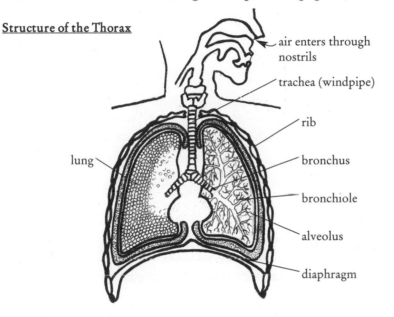

Structure of the Thorax

- air enters through nostrils
- trachea (windpipe)
- rib
- bronchus
- bronchiole
- alveolus
- diaphragm
- lung

Effects of smoking

Tobacco contains a drug called **nicotine**.
There is increased risk of heart disease because nicotine:
- speeds up the heart rate
- raises blood pressure.

Other problems are caused when tobacco is smoked. The lungs have a mechanism to keep themselves clean. This involves producing a layer of mucus that is moved up and down the throat by moving hairs called **cilia**. Smoking slows down the movement of the cilia and produces more mucus. This collects in the bronchioles (tiny tubes in the lungs) causing a 'smoker's cough'.

Micro-organisms can more easily get into the lungs making diseases such as bronchitis more common. If this is not cleared up, permanent damage to the lungs can occur.

Smoking also increases the chances of lung cancer.

Even not smoking does not remove all of the risks of tobacco. It has been shown that breathing in smoke from a nearby smoker, known as 'passive smoking', can lead to certain health risks.

Effects of alcohol

When alcohol is swallowed it quickly gets into the bloodstream. In small amounts it can reduce inhibitions and boost confidence. However, alcohol is a depressant drug that slows down the drinker's reactions. Co-ordination is clumsier and the vision can be impaired.

Effects of drugs

Like tobacco and alcohol, other drugs can affect the nervous system, which controls the operation of the body. There are four types of drug:

1. **Sedatives**, which slow the brain down and make the person sleepy.
2. **Stimulants**, which speed up the brain and make the person more alert.
3. **Hallucinogens** cause a person to have experiences that are different from real-life.
4. **Painkillers**, which remove our sense of pain.

Drugs can seriously affect health and can be addictive.

Breathing rate and depth

The breathing rate (number of breaths per minute) and the depth of breathing (volume of gas in dm^3 breathed out in each breath) are good measures of how much air is taken into the lung for gaseous exchange. There are two measures for the depth of breathing:

1. **Tidal volume.** The volume of air breathed in and out in normal breathing.
2. **Vital capacity.** The volume of air breathed in and out when deep breaths are taken and an attempt is made to expel all the air.

There is always some air left in the lungs that cannot be expelled.

? ? ? ? Questions ? ? ? ?

1. Why is the best advice to a driver to drink no alcohol?

2. Coffee, tea and some soft drinks contain caffeine. This is a stimulant. Why is a tired driver advised to drink coffee and then sleep for 15 minutes?

3. This table gives the results of some tests on an athlete.

Activity	Tidal volume in dm^3	Breaths per minute
sitting	0.6	15
standing	0.7	15
walking	1.2	18
running	1.8	21

   a. Suggest two ways the athlete gets more oxygen into the lungs when running.

   b. Why is it important that the athlete gets more oxygen into the lungs when running?

   c. What volume of air is taken into the lungs when walking for 5 minutes?

4. The air we breathe in travels along a pathway.
   Put the following in the correct order starting with the nose.
   alveoli   bronchioles   bronchus   nose   trachea

The skeleton and joints

A **skeleton** consists of large numbers of bones joined together.
Where bones join together is called a **joint.**
Some **joints** allow movement and others do not.

Joints at the hip, elbow and wrist allow us to move our bodies. Those in the skull are fixed; they are there to allow the skull to grow.

Joints at Hip and Knee

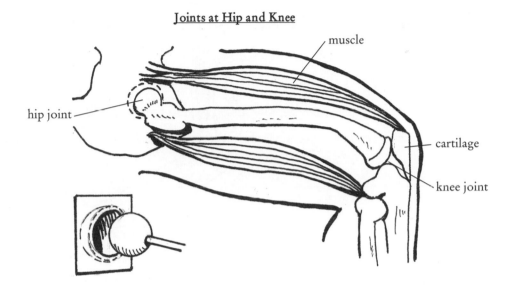

There are two types of joint shown in the diagram above:
- **ball-and-socket joint** e.g. the joint at the hip
- **hinge joint** e.g. the joint at the knee.

There is movement in all direction at the hip but only movement in one direction at the knee.

Joints also have:
- **cartilage** – a rubbery tissue on the surface of the bones where they rub together, lubricated by an oily liquid between the layers
- **muscles** – these can pull to move the leg.

Muscles move bones by contracting so that they pull on the bone.

KEY FACT: Muscles cannot push, they can only pull.
When a muscle is not exerting a pulling force it is **relaxed**.

Antagonistic pairs

A single muscle can only pull along its length, so it can only cause movement in one direction.
Two muscles are needed to raise and lower an arm.
These are the **biceps** and **triceps**. Because they act in opposite directions, the biceps and triceps are known as an **antagonistic pair** of muscles.

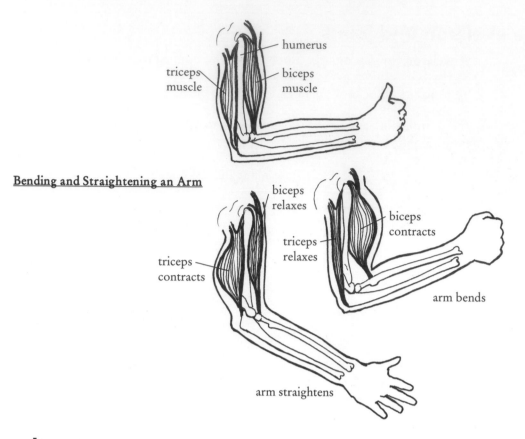

Bending and Straightening an Arm

Muscles as levers

Many muscles in the body act as **levers** that **magnify distance**. When the lower arm is raised or lowered, the elbow acts as the pivot. The muscle is attached to the bone very close to the pivot, so a large force is needed to produce the required moment (turning effect).

? ? ? ? Questions ? ? ? ?

1. a. Write down the names of three joints in the arm.

   b. Which joint is a ball and socket joint?

2. a. What type of tissue causes movement of the skeleton?

   b How does it do this?

3. a. What are an **antagonistic pair** of muscles?

   b. Name a pair of antagonistic muscles in the arm.

28. Plants and Photosynthesis

Animals cannot make their own food. Plants can make their own food by photosynthesis. This diagram shows the parts of a plant.

Parts of a Plant

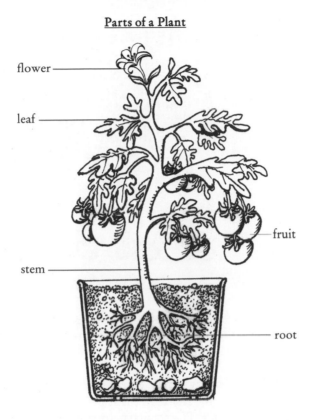

The roots of the plant:
- anchor the plant in the soil
- take water and dissolved minerals from the soil.

The water and dissolved minerals travel through hollow tubes in the stems to the leaves.

In the leaves the plants make food by **photosynthesis**.

Photosynthesis involves the reaction of water and carbon dioxide to produce glucose and oxygen. The oxygen is released into the atmosphere and the glucose.
This process takes place in sunlight and in the presence of the green pigment, chlorophyll, which is a catalyst.

The word equation for the reaction is:

$$\textbf{Carbon dioxide + water} \xrightarrow{\text{chlorophyll}} \textbf{glucose + oxygen}$$

The symbol equation for this process is:
$$6CO_2 + 6H_2O \rightarrow C_6H_{12}O_6 + 6O_2$$

The glucose can be stored in the plant as starch.
Green plants release oxygen back into the atmosphere.

Plants and Photosynthesis

What happens in the leaf?

This diagram shows a cross section through a leaf.

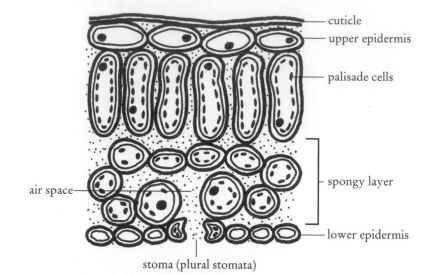

Leaves usually:
- have a large area to absorb the maximum amount of light
- are thin so that carbon dioxide does not have to travel far through the leaf
- have veins to give some support and provide the leaf with a supply of water.

Carbon dioxide needed for photosynthesis enters through the **stomata** (singular **stoma**). Most of the stomata are on the underside of the leaf. Stomata open and close. Oxygen and water escape through the stomata. The stomata close at night to prevent too much loss of water.

The waxy layer on the surface of the leaf, called the **cuticle**, prevents evaporation of water from the surface. Below the cuticle there is a single layer of tightly fitting cells called the **epidermis**. The **palisade cells**, below the epidermis but still near the surface of the leaf, contain a large number of **chloroplasts**. Chloroplasts contain the chlorophyll, and it is here that photosynthesis occurs.

The spongy layer contains large cells with irregular shapes. There are large gaps between the cells. Oxygen and carbon dioxide can be stored here.

Minerals needed for plant growth

Plants need large amounts of nitrogen, phosphorus and potassium if they are to grow well. This table shows how these three elements are used in the growing plant.

Element	Importance of the element to a growing plant
nitrogen, N	necessary for the growth of stems and leaves
phosphorus, P	essential for root growth
potassium, K	needed for the production of flowers

Other elements, including magnesium, sulphur and calcium, are needed in smaller amounts. Some elements, called **trace elements**, are needed in very small amounts.

Magnesium is needed for photosynthesis. If soil does not have enough magnesium in it, the plant cannot make enough chlorophyll. The plant is able to absorb less sunlight and does not grow. It does not make enough food and gives a low yield.

As plants grow they use up supplies of these elements in the soil. They can be added using **fertilisers**.

Growing plants in greenhouses

This table gives some advantages and disadvantages of growing plants in a greenhouse.

Advantages	Disadvantages
higher temperature than outside	pests and diseases can build up
crops grown earlier and later than outside	costs of greenhouse
controlled conditions	running costs
less wind damage	
increasing carbon dioxide for example from burning fuel in greenhouse heaters	

Farmers often use polytunnels to grow plants to yield early crops. Polythene sheeting stretched across a frame gives protection to growing plants.

Controlling pests

Predator – prey relationships

Gardeners with rose bushes may find that aphids called greenfly are causing problems. They multiply at a tremendous rate and damage the buds.
Gardeners may buy a **pesticide** to kill the aphids. A pesticide that kills insects is called an **insecticide**.

Aphids have a natural predator – the ladybird. Ladybirds kill huge numbers of aphids. However, using an insecticide also kills the ladybirds.

? ? ? ? Questions ? ? ? ?

1. A fertiliser is called an NPK fertiliser.
   What three essential elements does this fertiliser supply?

2. Choose two compounds from the list that could make an NPK fertiliser if mixed.
   calcium chloride   potassium nitrate   sodium phosphate

3. Which two advantages in growing plants in a greenhouse result in more photosynthesis?

4. Early potatoes may be grown under a polytunnel but the main crop will be grown in open fields.
   a. Why is a polytunnel used?

   b. Suggest why pests may be a more serious problem in polytunnels than open fields.

   c. Why are the main crop potatoes grown in open fields?

   d. Suggest two reasons why farmers are advised not to keep growing the same crops in the same field year after year.

29. Metals

You will be familiar with many metals and will appreciate the wide range of uses metals have. Over the past hundred years, metals have become more expensive as demand for them has increased and supplied are limited.

Scientists and engineers have developed new materials to replace metals for many uses.

Typical properties of metals

Metals are usually
- hard
- strong
- have high density
- have high melting points
- good conductors of heat energy and electrical energy
- malleable (can be beaten into thin sheets)
- ductile (can be drawn into wires).

Uses of metals

Different metals have different uses. This table gives some uses of metals.

Use	Metal	Reason for use
car body	steel (an alloy of iron)	strong; can be made into sheets
aeroplane	aluminium alloy	low density; strong
electricity cables	pure aluminium	good conductor of electricity
pylons	steel	strong
flashing on house roof	lead	unreactive; soft so that it can be shaped
ladder	aluminium alloy	low density; strong

Looking at these uses, there are different reasons why a particular metal is used. The following points are worth remembering:
- In many cases a mixture of metals, called an **alloy**, is used rather than a pure metal. Steel is an alloy of iron with a small amount of carbon alloy. Aluminium alloy is much stronger than pure aluminium.
- Metals are often used because they are good **conductors of electricity**. Pure aluminium is a better conductor of electricity than aluminium alloy. The fact that aluminium alloy is stronger is not relevant. The best conductor of electricity is silver but it is not used widely for conducting electricity because it is too expensive.
- Metals are also **good conductors of heat**. Metals are used to make radiators in houses.
- Unreactive metals, such as gold, platinum and silver, are used for jewellery.

Reactions of metals with acids

Dilute acids react with some metals to produce a **salt** and **hydrogen** gas.
This table shows how the salt produced depends upon the acid used.

Acid used	Salt produced
hydrochloric acid	chloride
sulphuric acid	sulphate
nitric acid	nitrate

Examples of reactions involving metals and acids are:
magnesium + hydrochloric acid → magnesium chloride + hydrogen
$Mg + 2HCl \rightarrow MgCl_2 + H_2$

zinc + sulphuric acid → zinc sulphate + hydrogen
$Zn + H_2SO_4 \rightarrow ZnSO_4 + H_2$

Hydrogen can be produced from magnesium and hydrochloric acid. We can test for hydrogen by putting a **lighted splint** into a test tube. The hydrogen burns with a **squeaky pop**.

Metals

1. This table shows some properties of glass, copper, aluminium and stainless steel.

Property	Glass	Copper	Aluminium	Stainless Steel
good conductor of heat				
good conductor of electricity				
high density	✓	✓	✓	✓
high melting point				
shiny				
reacts with an alkali	x	x	✓	x

a. Which material in the list is an alloy?

b. Complete the table with ✓ and x in each space.

c. Which material is least suitable for making a saucepan? Explain your choice.

d. The handle of a saucepan is often made of wood or plastic. Which material would be suitable for making the handle? Explain your choice.

e. Which material should not be used to make a saucepan which will often be washed frequently with a strong alkali?

2. Complete the word and symbol equations
   a. magnesium + sulphuric acid → _____ + _____
      $Mg + H_2SO_4$ → _____ + _____

   b. zinc + hydrochloric acid → _____ + _____
      $Zn + 2HCl$ → _____ + _____

   c. magnesium + nitric acid → _____ + _____
      $Mg + 2HNO_3$ → _____ + _____

   d. iron + _____ → iron chloride + _____
      Fe + _____ → $FeCl_2$ + _____

93

30. Reactions of Metal Oxides and Hydroxides with Acids

Metal oxides react with acids to form a salt and water only.
Hydrochloric acid is used to make chlorides, sulphuric acid makes sulphates and nitric acid makes nitrates.

For example: Copper (II) oxide + sulphuric acid $\rightarrow$ copper (II) sulphate + water
$$CuO + H_2SO_4 \rightarrow CuSO_4 + H_2O$$

Zinc oxide + hydrochloric acid $\rightarrow$ zinc chloride + water
$$ZnO + 2HCl \rightarrow ZnCl_2 + H_2O$$

Metal hydroxides react with an acid to form a salt and water only.

For example: sodium hydroxide + hydrochloric acid $\rightarrow$ sodium chloride + water
$$NaOH + HCl \rightarrow NaCl + H_2O$$

sodium hydroxide + sulphuric acid $\rightarrow$ sodium sulphate + water
$$2NaOH + H_2SO_4 \rightarrow Na_2SO_4 + 2H_2O$$

sodium hydroxide + nitric acid $\rightarrow$ sodium nitrate + water
$$NaOH + HNO_3 \rightarrow NaNO_3 + H_2O$$

25 cm^3 of sodium hydroxide solution is added to the conical flask. A pH meter probe is put into the solution. The pH reading is 13.

Hydrochloric acid is added drop by drop until the solution turns green. The solution is now neutral.

The solution is evaporated to recover the salt, sodium chloride.

Reactions of metal carbonates with acids

Metal carbonates react with acids to form a salt, water and carbon dioxide.
For example:
   Calcium carbonate + hydrochloric acid $\rightarrow$ calcium chloride + water + carbon dioxide
$$CaCO_3 + 2HCl \rightarrow CaCl_2 + H_2O + CO_2$$
   Sodium carbonate + sulphuric acid $\rightarrow$ sodium sulphate + water + carbon dioxide
$$Na_2CO_3 + H_2SO_4 \rightarrow Na_2SO_4 + H_2O + CO_2$$

In both cases, you would see fizzing as bubbles of colourless gas escape. This gas is carbon dioxide. You could show by bubbling the gas through limewater. The limewater turns cloudy (like milk) showing the carbon dioxide is present.

If you drop an Alka Seltzer tablet into water you will notice that it fizzes a lot. This gas is carbon dioxide. The tablet contains both an acid and a carbonate. When added to water they react and carbon dioxide is produced. They cannot react if water is not there.

 KEY POINT: Carbonate-acid reactions are very common especially reactions involving calcium carbonate.

Reactions of Metal Oxides and Hydroxides with Acids

? ? ? ? Questions ? ? ? ?

1. Finish the following word equations:

   a. zinc oxide + sulphuric acid → _____ + _____

   b. copper (II) oxide + hydrochloric acid → _____ + _____

   c. potassium hydroxide + nitric acid → _____ + _____

   d. magnesium oxide + sulphuric acid → _____ + _____

   e. calcium hydroxide + hydrochloric acid → _____ +_____

2. Write symbol equations for the reactions in question 1.

3. What name is given to reactions between acids and alkalis?

4. Finish the following word and symbol equations.
   a. Calcium carbonate + nitric acid → _____ _____ + _____

   + _____ _____

   $CaCO_3 + 2HNO_3 → Ca(NO_3)_2 +$ _____ + _____

   b. Potassium carbonate + sulphuric acid → _____ _____ + _____

   + _____ _____

   $K_2CO_3 + H_2SO_4 →$ _____ + _____ + _____

   c. Potassium carbonate + nitric acid → _____ _____ + _____

   + _____ _____

   $K_2CO_3 +$ __$HNO_3 →$ _____ + _____ + _____

5. Why should tablets such as Alka Seltzer be kept in containers with a tight lid?

31. Salts

Salts are compounds formed when an acid reacts with a metal, metal oxide, metal hydroxide or metal carbonate. They are formed when hydrogen in an acid is replaced by a metal.

e.g.

HCl	$\rightarrow$	$NaCl$
hydrochloric acid		sodium chloride
H_2SO_4	$\rightarrow$	Na_2SO_4
sulphuric acid		sodium sulphate
HNO_3	$\rightarrow$	$NaNO_3$
nitric acid		sodium nitrate
H_2CO_3	$\rightarrow$	Na_2CO_3
carbonic acid		sodium carbonate

Sodium chloride, sodium sulphate, sodium nitrate and sodium carbonate are **salts**.

Examples
1. From metals

zinc + sulphuric acid $\rightarrow$ zinc sulphate + hydrogen

$Zn + H_2SO_4 \rightarrow ZnSO_4 + H_2$

2. From metal oxides

copper (II) oxide + sulphuric acid $\rightarrow$ copper(II) sulphate + water

$CuO + H_2SO_4 \rightarrow CuSO_4 + H_2O$

3. From metal hydroxides

sodium hydroxide + hydrochloric acid $\rightarrow$ sodium chloride + water

$NaOH + HCl \rightarrow NaCl + H_2O$

4. From metal carbonates

calcium carbonate + hydrochloric acid $\rightarrow$ calcium chloride + water + carbon dioxide

$CaCO_3 + 2HCl \rightarrow CaCl_2 + H_2O + CO_2$

This table gives the names, formulae and uses of some common salts.

Chemical name	Formula	Common name	Use
sodium chloride	$NaCl$	common salt	flavouring and preserving food
sodium carbonate	$Na_2CO_3.10H_2O$	washing soda	chemical raw material, softening water
sodium sulphate	$Na_2SO_4.10H_2O$	Glauber's salts	medicine
potassium nitrate	KNO_3	saltpetre	making gunpowder
magnesium sulphate	$MgSO_4.7H_2O$	Epsom salt	laxative
sodium stearate	Complicated		soap

Making soluble salts

Salts that are soluble in water are produced when dilute acids react with metals, metal oxides, metal hydroxides and metal carbonates.

Copper (II) sulphate crystals can be produced from the reaction of copper (II) oxide with dilute sulphuric acid.

Copper (II) oxide + sulphuric acid → copper (II) sulphate + water

$CuO + H_2SO_4 \rightarrow CuSO_4 + H_2O$

Note:

- A frequent mistake is to write that the solution is saturated with copper (II) oxide. This assumes that the copper (II) oxide is dissolving. It is reacting. The reaction stops when all the acid is used up.
- Filtering removes excess copper (II) oxide.
- Evaporating the solution to dryness would decompose the copper (II) sulphate crystals.

? ? ? ? Questions ? ? ? ?

1. Magnesium sulphate can be prepared from reacting four different solids with sulphuric acid.

   a. Write down the names of the four possible starting materials.

   _____

   _____

   b. Write down the word and symbol equations for the four reactions.

   _____

   _____

   _____

   _____

   c. Put the five steps in the correct order.

   A. Leave to cool.

   B. Heat some dilute sulphuric acid.

   C. Filter off excess solid.

   D. Heat the solution until a small volume of solution remains.

   E. Add the solid in small portions to warm dilute sulphuric acid until some remains unreacted.

32. Environmental Issues

Role of chemists

People often think that chemists produce new materials without any thought for the environment around us. They are, however, very anxious to maintain and improve the environment.

Acid rain

Acid rain causes many environmental problems.

Rain water is naturally slightly acidic because carbon dioxide dissolves in water forming carbonic acid.

Water + carbon dioxide → carbonic acid
$$H_2O + CO_2 → H_2CO_3$$

However, the burning of fossil fuels, such as coal, produces **sulphur dioxide** in addition to other gases. Sulphur dioxide dissolves in water forming **sulphurous acid**. This is oxidised to form **sulphuric acid**.

water + sulphur dioxide → sulphurous acid
$$H_2O + SO_2 → H_2SO_3$$

sulphurous acid + oxygen → sulphuric acid
$$H_2SO_3 + O_2 → 2H_2SO_4$$

Vehicle exhausts produce **oxides of nitrogen** (sometimes written as NO). These dissolve in water to form **nitric acid**.

Causes of acid rain include coal fires, power stations and vehicle emissions from cars and lorries.

Consequences of acid rain

1. Damage to stonework on buildings. Buildings, especially in cities, have shown damage due to acid rain. A black skin first appears on the stone. This then blisters and cracks, causing the stone to be seriously disfigured. Buildings such as churches and cathedrals that have been standing for hundreds of years often show damage.

2. Rivers and lakes can become more acidic as acidic gases dissolve in the water. This kills wildlife including fish and otters. There are many lakes in Norway or Sweden that now have no animal life.

3. Forests are seriously damaged. Forests in Scandinavia and Germany especially are being damaged by acid rain. Trees are stunted, needles and leaves drop off and the trees die. It has been estimated that acid rain is costing the German forestry industry about £250 million each year.

4. Human life can be affected. Acid conditions can alter levels of copper, lead and aluminium in the body. These changes have been linked with diarrhoea in small babies and breathing disorders. There are many more cases of asthma which may be linked to sulphur dioxide and oxides of nitrogen in the atmosphere.

5. Damage to metalwork. Acid rain can speed up corrosion of metals. Wrought iron railings in city areas can show considerable damage.

Monitoring air and water pollution

Monitoring levels of pollution in air and water is important in detecting changes in pollutants over a period of time. In Great Britain about 50 years ago levels of air pollutants were much higher than they are today. In cities there were frequent serious fogs produced by soot ash and tar from the burning of coal in houses and factories. This fog was nicknamed **smog** and caused 4000 extra deaths in one winter alone in Great Britain.

The Clean Air Act (1956) set up clean air zones where coal could not be burned, only 'smokeless fuels'. As a result of this act and the careful monitoring of air pollution the situation in cities has improved.

Global warming

You have probably heard stories about the Earth warming up and some of the effects this might have on climates around the world. This is called **global warming** and is caused by the **greenhouse effect**.

In a greenhouse plants are kept warm. Short wavelength light energy from the Sun enters through the glass and warms up the inside of the greenhouse. The objects in the greenhouse radiate long wavelength infrared radiation but this cannot escape back out through the glass. The temperature then rises inside the greenhouse.

The Earth acts in a similar way but, instead of glass, there are gases in the atmosphere (carbon dioxide and methane) that do the same job. These gases let the short wavelength energy from the Sun in. The Earth is heated up and this re-radiates long wavelength energy. This radiation cannot escape and the temperature of the Earth and its atmosphere heat up.

Global Warming

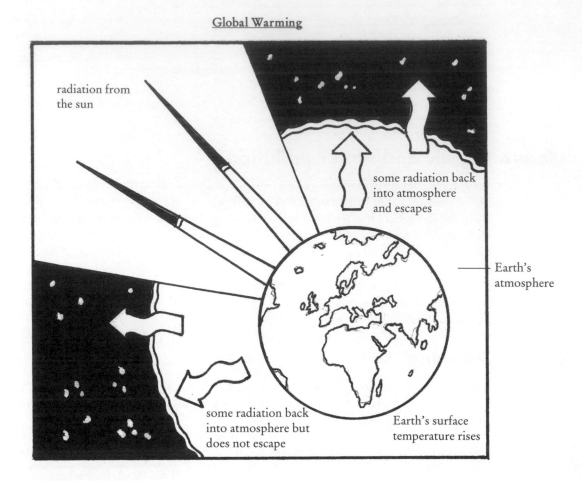

Effects of global warming

We need some degree of global warming to make conditions on the Earth suitable for human life. Without the greenhouse effect the surface of the Earth would be too cold. The problem of global warming comes about because the concentrations of carbon dioxide, in particular, are rising and the effect is getting greater and surface temperatures are rising.

Possible effects of global warming are:
• rising temperatures on the Earth's surface
• melting of glaciers and ice caps leading to rising sea levels. This would cause some islands e.g. Seychelles and countries e.g. Bangladesh to be completely flooded.
• rising ocean temperatures which may affect plankton growth
• changes of climate in different parts of the world. In the United Kingdom the climate might become more Mediterranean but winters could be wetter with strong winds.

Much of the problem of global warming could be reduced if less fossil fuels such as coal, oil and gas were burned. There could be a move from burning fossil fuels to generating electricity from wind, waves, solar power etc.

In many parts of the world there are deposits of methane hydrate. This, when melted, could provide vast amounts of fossil fuel. Using this source will produce more greenhouse gases and make the greenhouse effect worse. Raising the temperature of the Earth will melt more methane hydrate and release methane into the atmosphere.

Environmental Issues

1. Choose two gases from the list that cause acid rain.
   carbon dioxide   methane   nitrogen dioxide   oxygen   sulphur dioxide

2. Write down the names of two gases producing global warming.

3. Sulphur dioxide can be removed from the waste gases in a power station chimney.
   Write down the name of a substance that will remove sulphur dioxide.

4. In a car engine some nitrogen and oxygen combine to form oxides of nitrogen. One of
   these oxides of nitrogen is nitrogen dioxide, NO_2.

   a. Write a word equation for the reaction forming nitrogen dioxide in the car engine.

   b. Complete the symbol equation for this reaction.
      $$N_2 + O_2 \rightarrow NO_2$$
   c. Nitrogen dioxide dissolves in water in the presence of oxygen to form nitric acid.
      Write down word and symbol equations for this reaction.

5. a. Why could methane hydrate deposits be of enormous value?

   b. What problem is caused when large amounts of methane are burned?

   c. What effect would that have on the deposits of methane hydrate?

33. Energy Transfer

Energy transfer

Every event involves **energy** and an **energy transfer**.
Things we use every day transfer energy.
Here are some examples:

A kettle transfers energy from **electricity** to **heat** in the water.

An electric light bulb transfers energy from **electricity** to **light**.

A dynamo on a bicycle transfers **energy of movement** into **electricity**

A solar cell in a calculator transfers energy from **light** into **electricity**.

A loudspeaker transfers energy from **electricity** to **sound**.

Other ways in which objects have energy include:
- gravitational potential energy – this is the type of energy that an object gains when it moves uphill
- chemical energy – the energy stored in fuels and in batteries.

Generating electricity

Only small amounts of electricity can be stored in rechargeable batteries. This is useful for starting a car or for emergency electrical supplies.
Generally, electricity cannot be stored. It has to be generated as it is needed.

Most of our energy is generated using **fossil fuels**.

This diagram below shows how a coal-burning power station produces electricity.-

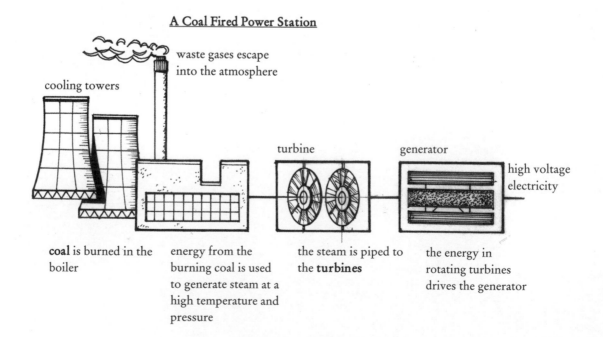

A Coal Fired Power Station

waste gases escape into the atmosphere

cooling towers

turbine

generator

high voltage electricity

coal is burned in the boiler

energy from the burning coal is used to generate steam at a high temperature and pressure

the steam is piped to the **turbines**

the energy in rotating turbines drives the generator

Inside the generator an electromagnet spins inside thick copper conductors. The movement of the magnetic field causes a voltage and a current in the copper conductors. This generates electricity.

Nuclear power stations operate in a similar way:
- nuclear fuel is contained in a reactor
- energy is released when large atomic nuclei are split into smaller ones
- the energy is removed by a coolant and used to keep turbines spinning.

Governments are being encouraged to generate electricity from renewable sources to reduce damage to the environment (see Unit 32).

Energy flow

When a kettle is used to heat some water, the kettle and its contents are gaining energy as they warm up.
When a lamp is used to light a room, energy **flows** through the lamp at a constant rate.
All the energy that flows into the lamp also flows out – this is known as **conservation of energy**.
Energy is never created or destroyed – this is the principle of conservation of energy.

If you turn off a light at the mains switch, the room goes dark immediately.
The transfer of energy is taking place all the time when the lamp is on.
Light doesn't stay as light for very long after leaving the lamp, so the light in a room has to be continually replaced. What happens to the energy that leaves the lamp?
- The hot lamp loses energy to the surrounding air – this is carried away by a convection current.
- The light and infra-red radiation are absorbed by the walls and other surfaces – causing them to warm up.

Spreading energy around

When a lamp is being used to light a room, all the energy from the lamp is spread out or **dissipated** in the room. This causes a very small temperature rise.

The diagram below shows the energy emitted from a television set. Warm air rises from the back of the television. This heats the air in the room. The energy emitted as sound and light is absorbed by the walls and furnishings.

Almost all the energy that we take from sources such as electricity, gas, coal and petrol ends up as heat in our surroundings – in the buildings that we live in, the air and the outdoors.

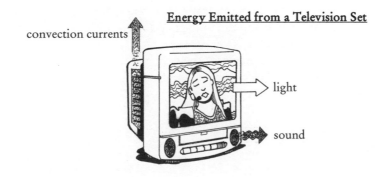

convection currents

Energy Emitted from a Television Set

light

sound

Once this energy has been spread out we cannot get this energy back very easily. It is much easier to get more energy from a fuel or electricity than to extract the energy from the air and the ground outside.

Energy in circuits

A torch has to be portable, so it uses batteries for its energy supply.
Milk floats also use batteries which are recharged from the electricity mains supply overnight. When a torch is being used:
- chemical reactions take place in the battery
- these reactions release energy
- the electric current transfers the energy to the lamp.

A milk float needs much more energy than a torch does. It uses batteries that have a higher **voltage**.
The bigger the battery voltage, the greater the energy transferred by a given current.

Measuring voltage

Batteries can have different voltages e.g. 1.5V, 3V or 9V.
Laboratory power supplies usually have different voltage settings.

The diagrams show how a **voltmeter** is used to measure the voltage of a power supply and across one of the lamps in a series circuit.

<u>Using a Voltmeter to Measure Voltage</u>

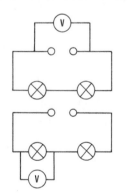

A voltmeter is a device that measures voltage in **volts** (V).
It is always connected in **parallel** with a power supply or component.

Voltage is a measure of the energy transfer to and from the charged particles that carry the current in a circuit. Increasing the voltage in the circuit shown above increases the brightness of the lamps. This is because:
- increasing the voltage increases the current
- the moving charged particles have more energy to transfer from the power supply to the lamps.

? ? ? ? Questions ? ? ? ?

1. Why are power stations usually serviced and repaired during the summer?

2. In which part of the power station:
   a. is fuel burned?
   b. is steam generated?
   c. is electricity produced?

3. This diagram shows the energy transfer in a low energy bulb.

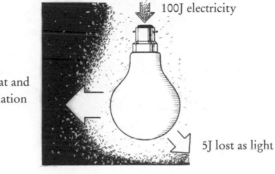

   a. Explain how the principle of conservation of energy applies to the low energy bulb shown in the diagram.
   b. Explain why low energy bulbs may be worth using despite the fact they cost more than ordinary bulbs.

4. The table gives information about energy wasted in a coal-fired power station.

Place where energy is wasted	Percentage wasted
boiler	15
cooling tower	45
generator	5

   All of the rest of the energy is transferred to electricity. What is the percentage of energy transferred to electricity?

5. What is the relationship between the supply voltage and the current that passes?

34. Gravitational Forces

Gravitational force

The Moon goes round the Earth and the Earth goes round the Sun. This rotation is due to the **gravitational force** that exists between any two objects.

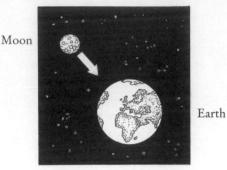

If you tie a rubber bung onto the end of a piece of string you can whirl it round your head in a circle; but it only keeps going round you as long as you are pulling on the string. If you let go of the string the bung carries on moving, but its horizontal motion is in a straight line. There needs to be a constant pulling force acting on an object to make it follow a circular path.

<u>Swinging a Rubber Bung in a Circle</u>

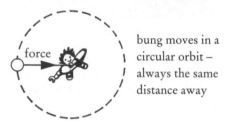

bung moves in a circular orbit – always the same distance away

The motion of planets in the solar system is due to the gravitational pulling forces between the Sun and the planets.

The Sun's gravitational pull

This diagram shows the relative strength of the Sun's gravitational pull on Mercury, Venus and Earth.

<u>Gravitational Attraction Keeps Planets in Orbit</u>

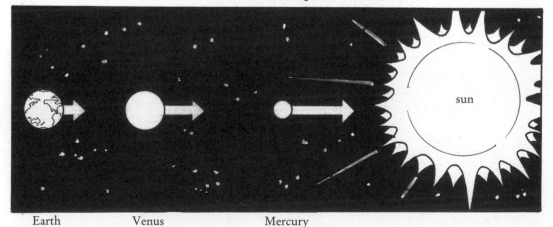

The Sun's gravitational pull keeps the planets in orbit.

The strength of the Sun's gravitational pull is weaker on planets further away. The strength of the Sun's gravitational pull determines the speed of a planet in its orbit.

KEY FACT: The closer a planet is to the Sun, the greater the strength of the Sun's gravitational pull and the faster the planet moves.

Gravitational forces:
- act between all objects that have mass
- increase in strength with increasing mass
- decrease in strength with increasing separation of the masses.

Orbits of the planets

All the planets move in orbits that are **elliptical**. This means that sometimes they are closer to the Sun than other times. For all the planets except Mercury the ellipses are very near to being circles so the distance between the Earth and the Sun does not change very much during a year.
Mercury's orbit takes it closer to the Sun at some times of its year and this affects its speed.

As Mercury gets closer to the Sun, it speeds up in its orbit and it slows down as it gets further away.

At Jupiter, the strength of the Sun's pull is even weaker than at the Earth, but the actual force that pulls Jupiter towards the Sun is bigger than that pulling the Earth; this is because Jupiter is more massive than the Earth so there is a lot more matter for the Sun to pull on! Jupiter still moves more slowly than the Earth because the **mass** of a planet does not affect the speed of its orbit. It is the **distance** from the Sun that is important.

Satellites

The Sun's pull keeps the planets going round it. In the same way the Earth's pull keeps the Moon moving around the Earth.
The Moon is the Earth's **natural satellite**.
There are hundreds of artificial satellites around the Earth that do a wide variety of jobs.
Satellites are used:
- to take **photographs** of the Earth at regular intervals so that weather forecasters can see the changes in **weather patterns**
- for **television broadcasting** and for communicating by telephone and radio between places that are 'hidden' by the Earth's curvature
- by ships, cars and aircraft for **navigating**
- by some countries to **spy** on others.

Gravitational Forces

1. The Moon is the Earth's natural satellite.
   a. What is a satellite?

   b. Write down two uses of artificial satellites.

   c. Underline two words that correctly describe the force acting on a satellite moving around the Earth.
      attractive   **frictional**   **gravitational**   **magnetic**   **repulsive**   **resistive**

   d. What factor determines the speed at which a satellite moves around the Earth?

2. a. How is the orbit of Mercury around the Sun different from the other planets?

   b. How does this affect the speed of movement of Mercury around the Sun?

35. Speed, Distance and Time

Winning the race

The 100m race is the highlight of an athletics competition.
The runners in this race run faster than in any other race.
The winner is the person who arrives at the finish in the shortest time.
Measured over the whole race, the person who takes the shortest time has the
greatest **speed**.

To work out the speed of a moving object two measurements are needed:
- the distance travelled by the object
- the time taken to travel that distance.

For example, Kim Collins runs 100m in 10.00s.
His average speed can be calculated using the equation:

$$\text{average speed} = \frac{\text{distance travelled}}{\text{time taken}}$$

$$v = \frac{s}{t}$$

$$= \frac{100}{10.00} \text{ m/s}$$

$$= 10.0 \text{ m/s}$$

Note that this is an average speed. At times during the race he may be running faster and at
other times he may be running slower.

Examples

Example 1
Calculate the average speed of a car that takes 5 seconds to travel 120 m.

Answer:
$$v = \frac{s}{t}$$

$$= \frac{120 \text{ m}}{5 \text{ s}}$$

$$= 24 \text{ m/s}.$$

The unit of speed here is m/s, because the distance is measured in m and the time is
measured in s. This is a common unit of speed.

Example 2
Calculate the average speed of a bus that travels 9.5 miles in 0.5 hours.

Answer:
$$v = \frac{s}{t}$$

$$= \frac{9.5 \text{ miles}}{0.5 \text{ hours}}$$

$$= 19 \text{ mph}$$

The unit "miles per hour" is normally written as mph rather than m/h.

How long does it take?

If you are walking to catch a bus or travelling to an airport or ferry port, you need to know

what time to set off so that you arrive in time. To estimate the time for a journey, two pieces of information are needed:
- the distance to travel
- the average speed.

In good weather conditions, provided there are no delays such as traffic jams, the average speed of a car travelling on a motorway is about 60 mph. How long would a journey of 150 miles take?

To answer this you need to be able to use the speed equation in the form "time = ...". The speed equation can be written in three different ways.
In symbols, these are:

$$v = \frac{s}{t} \qquad t = \frac{s}{v} \qquad s = v \times t$$

These are all different ways of writing the same equation.
The journey time can now be worked out.
Answer:
$$t = \frac{s}{v}$$
$$= 150 \text{ miles} \div 60 \text{ mph}$$
$$= 2.5 \text{ hours.}$$

Using graphs

Two types of line graph that are often used to show the motion of an object are:
- **distance-time** graphs; the distance travelled by an object can only increase with time.
- **speed-time** graphs; speed can increase and decrease so the line can go down as well as up.

Here are two graphs that show the same journey.

Two Graphs to Show the Same Journey

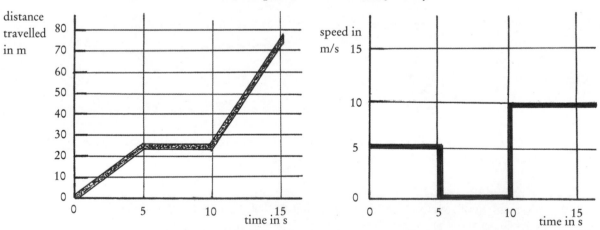

Both graphs show a constant speed of 5 m/s for the first 5 s, followed by a 5 s rest and then a constant speed of 10 m/s for the next 5 s. Notice how, on the distance-time graph, the steeper the line the greater the speed.

The **slope**, or **gradient**, of a distance-time graph represents **speed**.

KEY FACT: The greater the slope, the faster the object is moving.

110

Speed, Distance and Time

1. Look at the two graphs opposite.
   a. What is the total distance travelled in 15s?

   b. What is the average speed over the total journey?

2. A Boeing 747 flies 3750 miles at an average speed of 500 mph.
   a. Suggest at which points of the journey the plane is likely to be flying much slower than the average speed.

   b. Calculate the time of the flight.
                    Time _____ Unit _____

3. A cyclist cycles at an average speed of 10 m/s. He cycles for 2 minutes. What distance does he travel?

36. Pressure

Pressure

Three everyday examples of using a force to create a large pressure are:
- pushing a drawing pin into a board
- cutting food with a knife
- ice-skating.

Pressure is the force applied on unit area.

Pressure describes the effect a force has in **cutting** or **piercing** the surface it acts on:
- knives, scissors, needles and drawing pins are all designed to cut or pierce. They apply a force onto a small area and so produce a high pressure. This maximises the effect they have in cutting and piercing.
- skis and caterpillar tracks on heavy vehicles are examples of where a force is spread over a large area to reduce the pressure it causes. This minimises the effect they have in cutting and piercing.

Under greater pressure

Ice skaters do not skate on ice; they skate on water:
- an ice skater's weight pushes down on the small area of the blades
- the high pressure on the ice below the blades causes it to melt, so the blades are surrounded by a film of water
- the water re-freezes when the ice skate has passed.

This is how an ice skater leaves tracks in the ice; the tracks are where the ice has melted and then re-frozen.

Animals and pressure

Animals, when they walk on the ground, need to be able to do so without sinking. A heavy animal needs a large surface area of the feet in contact with the ground.
An elephant needs large feet to prevent it sinking.

Some animals, like squirrels and some birds, need to exert a large pressure so that they can grip the surface they walk on. They have claws. Claws push down on a small surface area so they produce a high pressure. The claws pierce and grip on the surface.

Calculating pressure

Pressure is calculated as the force acting on each cm² or m² of surface area using the relationship:

$$\text{Pressure} = \text{force} \div \text{area} \text{ or } P = \frac{F}{A}$$

Pressure is measured in N/m² or pascal (Pa) when the force is measured in N and the area is measured in m².
When the area involved is small and is measured in cm², the unit N/cm² is used.

Example 1
A bulldozer weighs 150 000 N. To stop it from sinking into the soft mud it moves on caterpillar tracks. The area of the tracks in contact with the ground is 10 m². Calculate the pressure on the ground.

Answer: Pressure = force ÷ area
                           = 150 000 N ÷ 10 m^2
                           = 15 000 Pa.

Example 2

A hammer hits a nail with a force of 200 N. The tip of the nail has a surface area of 0.005 cm^2. Calculate the pressure that the tip exerts.

Answer: Pressure = force ÷ area
                           = 200 N ÷ 0.005 cm^2
                           = 40 000 N/cm^2.

Like the speed equation, the pressure equation can be written in three different ways:

$$p = \frac{F}{A} \qquad F = p \times A \qquad A = \frac{F}{p}$$

So not only pressure, but also force and area can be calculated if the other two quantities are known.

Example 3

The pressure at the bottom of a pond is 200 000 Pa. Calculate the size of the force that pushes down on an area of 0.85 m^2.

Answer: Force = pressure × area
                          = 200 000 Pa × 0.85 m^2
                          = 170 000 N

? ? ? ? Questions ? ? ? ?

1. Complete the sentences using words from the list. The words can be used once, more than once or not at all.

   blunt   force   large   pressure   sharp   small

   A knife is _____ so that it exerts a force on a _____ surface area. This enables it to cause a large _____ .

   An Arctic explorer walking across snow wears snow shoes which have a _____ surface area. This means he exerts a _____ pressure and does not sink into the snow.

2. Calculate the pressure caused by:
   a. A force of 100 N that acts over an area of 4 m².

      Pressure = _____ Unit _____
   b. A 500 N force pushing on an area of 1.25 m².

      Pressure = _____ Unit _____
   c. A 300 N force pushing on an area of 0.2 cm².

      Pressure = _____ Unit _____

3. An ice skater has a weight of 600 N. She exerts a pressure of 1 200 000 Pa on the ice when skating on both skates. Calculate the total area of the blades of her ice skates.

   Area _____

4. Use the pressure equation to fill in the blanks in the table. Write down the correct unit in each case.

	Force	Area	Pressure
a	30 N	2 m²	
b		0.3 m²	600 Pa
c	80 N		500 Pa
d	250 N	0.2 m²	
e		2.5 m²	100 000 Pa
f	1000N	10 cm²	

37. Turning Forces

Forces are used when we turn something round, for example, when we turn on a tap or open a door.
The point that things turn around is called the **pivot**.

In the case of a tap, the pivot is at the centre of the tap; a door pivots around the hinge.

If you try closing a door by pushing it at different places, you realise why door handles are placed as far from the pivot as possible.

The effect that a force has in turning something round is called the **moment** of the force.
It depends on:
- the size of the force
- how far away from the pivot the force is applied.

The moment of a force is calculated using the relationship:

moment = force × perpendicular (shortest) distance to pivot

Example
A force of 100 N is used to push a door open.
The force acts at right angles to the door at a distance of 0.8 m from the hinges.
Calculate the moment (turning effect) of the force.

Answer: moment = force × perpendicular distance to pivot
            = 100 N × 0.8 m
            = 80 N m

Balancing a seesaw

A seesaw has two forces acting on it:

anticlockwise movement

clockwise movement

<u>When Balanced the Two Movements are Equal</u>

- Each force has a turning effect but these two forces are acting in opposition.
- If the moments of the forces are equal, the seesaw is balanced.
- If the moments are unequal the seesaw is not balanced.
- The seesaw moves down on the side where the moment is greatest.

This is the **principle of moments.**

This states that:

if an object is balanced, the sum of the clockwise moments about a pivot is equal to the sum of the anticlockwise moments about the same pivot.

Example
Calculate the size of the force *F* needed to balance the seesaw shown in the diagram.

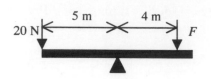

Answer: anticlockwise moment = 20 N x 5 m = 100 N m
clockwise moment = 100 N m, so *F* = 100 N m ÷ 4 m = 25 N

? ? ? ? Questions ? ? ? ?

1. State whether each seesaw is balanced, will tip to the right or tip to the left.

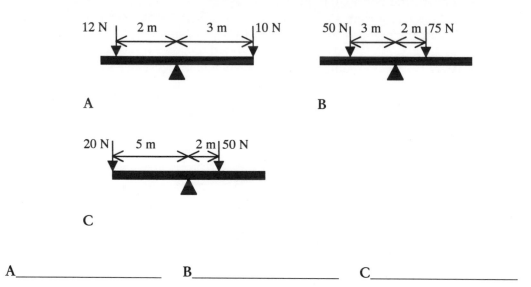

A_____   B_____   C_____

2. Calculate the size of the force *X* in the diagram if the rod is balanced.

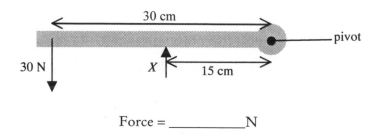

Force = _____N

3. Tim wants to change the wheel on his car. He jacks up the car and gets a spanner to loosen the wheel nuts. The wheel nuts will not turn. He gets a longer spanner and the wheel nuts turn. Explain why this happens.

Answers

1. Cells

1. a. No cell wall
      No chloroplasts
   b. Does not have a rigid cell wall around it.
   c. Nucleus
   d. To allow substances to pass easily in and out of the cell.
2. Cells Tissues Organs Systems
3. a. To absorb water and minerals into the plant.
   b. Long and thin (a large surface area)
   c. Chloroplasts

2. Reproduction and Adolescence

1. Reproduction without sex involving only one parent.
2. A male sex cell (e.g. sperm) and a female sex cell (e.g. egg).
3. Hair grows around the penis and on the scrotum. The penis grows larger.
4. Some plants can be grown from cuttings.
5. a. Cervix;   b. Ovary;   c. Uterus
6. a. 28 days;   b. The egg ripens;   c. In an ovary;   d. Between 13 and 15 days
   e. The lining of the uterus is thickening.
7. The lining of the uterus falls away and is lost through the vagina.

3. Fertilisation

1. A frog lays its eggs into a pond. The frog does not take any care of the eggs or the tadpoles produced.
   Many will die. A large number of eggs is needed to ensure a few survive and mature. Human females produce one egg each month . If fertilised this is allowed to develop inside the mother where it is protected and cared for.
2. A fetus is formed when the single cell produced in fertilisation divides several times. The fetus has recognisable human features.
3. a. i. Testes   ii. Ovaries
   b. Fertilisation.
   c. One.
4. Keep the embryo warm. Protect it from shock.

4. Feeding Relationships/Habitats

1. Where an animal or plant lives.
2. Food, shelter and a place to reproduce.
3. A tail – to enable the fish to swim in a particular direction.
   Fins – to let the fish move through the water.
   Gills – to enable the fish to take in oxygen from the water.
4. Three possibilities are
   Flowers → caterpillars → woodpeckers →kestrels
   Flowers → aphids → woodpeckers → kestrels
   Flowers → beetles → woodpeckers → kestrels
5. Water and carbon dioxide.
6. a. Carnivore;   b. Herbivore;   c. Omnivore
7. There is more light on the woodland floor in spring before the tree leaves open.

8. Large leaves. Float on the surface of the water.

5. Variation and Classification

1. Both. Pigment colour is inherited but may be affected by factors such as exposure to the Sun.
2. Frog, goldfish, monkey, sparrow
3. Vertebrates have backbones, invertebrates do not.
4. Mollusca
5. Mammalia give birth to live young.
6. They are both vertebrates.

6. Acids and Alkalis

1. A wasp injects alkali into the skin so an acid is needed to neutralise it . A bee injects acid into the skin and so it needs an alkali to neutralise it.
2. A tablet contains a known dose.
3. Add red and blue litmus paper.
   In hydrochloric acid both pieces of litmus paper turn red.
   In sodium hydroxide both pieces turn blue.
   In water one piece will be blue and one red.
4. Lithium hydroxide is an alkali. Alkalis are often hydroxides.
5. a. Bicarbonate of soda and sodium hydroxide;   b. 7;   c. Hydrogen
6. There is the same amount of acid in each beaker. Fewer tablets will be needed for the brand containing more alkali.
7. Add bicarbonate of soda to neutralise the acid and then wash away with plenty of water.

7. Making New Materials

1. a . chemical change; b. physical change; c. chemical change; d. physical change; e. physical change.
2. a. The candle continues to burn using up oxygen in the air. When the oxygen is used up the candle goes out.
   b. The candle would burn for longer before it goes out.
3. The metal combines with oxygen from the air to form an oxide and therefore increases in mass.
4. a. Hydrogen
   b. Carbon dioxide
   c. Calcium oxide
   d. Hydrochloric acid, hydrogen
   e. Sulphuric acid, water, carbon dioxide

8. States of Matter

1. The three states of matter are solid (ice), liquid (water) and gas (steam).
   Ice exists below 0°C. Water between 0°C and 100°C. Steam above 100°C.
2. a. Liquid;   b. Solid
3. a. Gas;   b. Solid;   c. Gas

9. Separating Mixtures

1. a. Three.
   b. Two
   c. If a pen was used, the ink would start to separate by chromatography.
2. The boiling points of the two liquids are too close together.

10. Fuels and Energy

1. 500 J
2. Less pollution. Supplies cannot run out.
3. Not necessary as alternative sources.
   Sun does not shine all day.
   Less electricity generated in winter when demand is highest.
4. a. Wind;   b. Moon
5. a. Hydroclectric.
   b. i. Pumping water back to the lake.
       ii. Storing water is easier than storing electricity.

11. Electricity

1. Nylon, polythene.
2. Series.
3. Parallel.
4. a. B
   b. In A both switches have to be closed to light the lamps. Then both lamps light. Not possible to have one lamp on.
   If a lamp 'blows' both lamps fail. In B both lamps can be turned on and off separately.
5. a. 2 A b. None.
6. To transfer energy from the power supply to the components.
7. Heat energy and light energy.
8. a. Series
   b. Change the speed of the motor.
9. A1 2.4 A; A2 1.2 A; A3 2.4A

12. Forces and their Effects

1. There is much greater resistance in water than in air.
2. The pull of the crane upward and the weight of the container downward.
3. 900N
4. a. Unbalanced. The driving force is greater than the resistive forces.
   b. The resistive forces increase.
   c. Balanced. The two forces are equal.
   d. Unbalanced. The resistive forces are greater than the driving forces.
5. There is not enough friction to stop the feet from slipping and sliding.
6. The metal ball has a greater weight. In the case of the metal ball the downward force is greater than the upthrust so it sinks. In the case of the wooden ball the downward force is less than the upthrust so it floats.
7. When she starts to jump the downward force due to weight is much greater than the upward force of air resistance. She speeds up. When she is falling at a constant speed, the two forces are balanced. When the parachute is opened the downward force is the same but the upward force is now much greater. She slows down.

8. They could make the car lighter. They could also make the design more streamlined to reduce air resistance.

13. The Earth and Beyond

1. a. Earth; b. Jupiter; c. Mercury; d. Saturn and Uranus
2. Mercury.
3. It is closest to the Sun so has to travel the shortest distance.
   It is travelling faster.
4. a. High densities.
   b. Jupiter. It has the highest gravitational pull.
   c. Much greater gravitation pull on Jupiter so it will take more energy to lift it if the surface of the planet.
   d. Venus is closer to the Earth than Mars is. It is also closer to the Sun so it is lit more brightly.
   e. Uranus
   f. Asteroids.
5. The Earth's rotation on its axis.
6. The Earth's tilt on its axis.
7. When the northern hemisphere is tilted towards the Sun, the southern hemisphere is tilted away from it.
8. Energy from the Sun is spread out over a smaller area of the Earth.
9. 366. One for each day and one for one revolution around the Sun.
10. 12 hours. Nights at least this length are needed to be able to see it.

14. Feeding and Digestion

1. Plants make their own food and therefore do not need to digest food from other sources. Exception would be carnivorous plants such as Venus fly trap.
2. Glucose; amino acid; glycerol and fatty acid.
3. Mouth, oesophagus, stomach, duodenum, small intestine, large intestine, rectum, anus.
4. The ileum is long and has a large surface area where absorption can take place.
5. Any three from : glucose, amino acid, glycerol and fatty acid.
6. Protein foods break up into amino acids which cannot be stored in the body. If they are not used they are excreted.
7. Pasta is rich in carbohydrate which breaks down into glucose. this provides energy.
8. Chewing bread breaks down starch in the mouth into glucose and hence the sweet taste.
9.

Test	A	B	C
protein test	blue solution	mauve colour	blue solution
starch test	blue-black colour	no blue-black colour	blue-black colour
simple sugar test	blue solution	blue solution	red-brown solid
fat test	clear	clear	milky white

15. Respiration

1. a. Both processes use oxygen, produce carbon dioxide and water. They also release energy.
   b. Burning releases some energy as light (a flame) but respiration does not.
2. glucose + oxygen → carbon dioxide + water + energy
3. a. To prove that there was no carbon dioxide in the air – all the carbon dioxide had been removed by the potassium hydroxide solution.
   b. Nothing.
   c. The limewater in the second flask goes cloudy faster.

16. Breathing in and out

1. Inhaled air contains more oxygen and less carbon dioxide than exhaled air.
2. Exhaled air is warmer and contains more water vapour.
3. a. So that oxygen can pass through into the bloodstream. Oxygen is needed by the muscles for respiration.
   b. Patient can be given air enriched with oxygen or pure oxygen to breathe.
   c. Mountaineers and astronauts.
4. The rib cage moves downwards and inwards.
   The diaphragm moves upwards.
   There is now less space inside the thorax.
   There is more pressure inside the thorax.
   This causes air to be pushed out of the lungs.

17. Microbes and Disease

1. Cytoplasm and cell membrane
2. No nucleus or cytoplasm
3. 100 minutes
4. The white blood cells produce antibodies that fight the bacteria. Some remain to fight another infection.
5. a. Antibiotics have no effect on viruses.
   b. Isolation of patients, destroying handkerchiefs etc.

18. Elements

1. a. carbon; b. phosphorus; c. magnesium; d. chlorine; e. zinc; f. potassium; g. mercury; h. lead; i. iron; j. manganese.
2. a. Metal; b. non-metal; c. non-metal; d. non-metal; e. metal; f. non-metal.
3. No, some non-metals have names ending in -ium e.g. selenium or helium.

19. Mixtures and Compounds

1. Nitrogen + hydrogen → nitrogen hydride (or ammonia)
2. This sample of acid is not pure or contains impurities.
3. a. Potassium, chlorine and oxygen
   b. Oxygen
   c. Potassium chlorate → potassium chloride + oxygen
4. Air is a mixture (variable composition) and water is a compound (fixed composition).

5. a. Copper (II) chloride.
   b. Copper (II) chloride and copper (II) oxide.
      NOT copper (II) hydroxide. The name ends in -ide but there are three elements present – copper, hydrogen and oxygen. This is an exception to the normal rules.
   c. Copper (II) hydroxide copper (II) sulphate and copper (II) nitrate.
   d. i. Oxygen
      ii. Copper (II) nitrate → copper (II) oxide + nitrogen dioxide + oxygen.

20. Rocks

1. Sedimentary   sandstone, shale, mudstone, limestone, conglomerate
   Metamorphic   marble, slate
   Igneous   granite, basalt
2. Granite has larger crystals because it has cooled slowly within the Earth. Basalt has smaller crystals because it has crystallised quickly on the surface of the Earth.
3. a. Marble and limestone.
   b. Granite – hard and attractive but not attacked by weather.
   c. Limestone, cheap and quite hard.
   d. Too slippery.
4. carbon dioxide + water → carbonic acid
   calcium carbonate + carbonic acid → calcium hydrogencarbonate

21. Moving Energy Around

1. Prevents loss of radiant energy.
   Trapped air in the bubbles is a good insulator. The air cannot move so no convection can take place.
2. Air is trapped between the layers of clothes and this is a good insulator.
3. Air is a poor conductor but if it is free to move it removes energy by forming convection currents.
4. It stops convection currents being set up in the cavity resulting in energy loss.
5. It prevents energy loss by evaporation and convection currents.
6. Air that has been warmed has a lower density. It rises and is replaced by cooler air with a higher density.

22. Magnets and Electromagnets

1. Iron and steel.
2. Repel, attract.
3. Pass the coins under an electromagnet. Steel coins plated with copper will be picked up but the alloy coins will not.
4. Steel retains its magnetism much longer than iron.
5. North-seeking pole or north pole.
6. The compass will point to the steel of the ship rather than magnetic north.
7. Inside the coil the magnetic field is from the south-seeking pole to the north. Outside the coil the magnetic field is from the north-seeking pole to the south.
8. Use same number of turns on the coil. Carry out five experiments with five different currents. Each time count how many paper clips are picked up.

9. The core becomes magnetised, the top of the armature is attracted to the core as the armature moves, it presses the switch contacts together.
10. The relay coil is operated by the low voltage sensing circuit. The relay contacts can be used to switch the mains.

23. Light

1. Luminous – candle flame, lit electric light bulb, Sun
   Non-luminous – aeroplane, moon
2. Metal object, wooden block.
3. Light travels in straight lines.
4. The speed of light is very much greater than the speed of sound.
5. Two eyes enable an accurate estimate of distance of an object to be made.

24. Sound and Hearing

1. 2000
2. a. 5; b. 100 Hz
3. Sound cannot pass through a vacuum as there are no particles.
4. Vibrations of the ear drum are transmitted through the ossicles to the inner ear. Messages are sent along the auditory nerve to the brain.
5. The greater the amplitude, the louder the sound.

25. Inheritance and Selection

1. a. Male sex cell (sperm) fuses with female sex cell (egg) to form a new cell called a zygote.
   b. In humans sperm cell and egg cell each contain 23 chromosomes and zygote contains 46 chromosomes (23 pairs).
   In general, sperm cell and egg cell contain half the number of genes in the zygote.
2. Taking cuttings will produce all plants identical in colour to the parents. The plants grown from seed will all be different. Some may be better than the original plants but some may not.
3.

Characteristic	Genetic	Environmental
natural colour of finger nails	✓	
colour of eyes	✓	
length of finger nails		✓
length of feet	✓	✓
length of hair	✓	✓

4. Home gardener – good flavour; a long season so they ripen a few at a time rather than all together.
Commercial grower – have thick skins that do not split easily when they are being transported; are uniform in colour, size and shape; have a long shelf life; ripen over a short period of time for cheaper harvesting.

26. Fitness

1. A person can never be sure what the level is. Drinking nothing is the only way to be certain.
2. Fifteen minutes to allow caffeine to get into the bloodstream. Caffeine acts as a stimulant and keeps the driver awake.
3. a. Higher tidal volume and more breaths per minute.
   b. Oxygen in the lungs moves into the blood stream. Oxygen is required for respiration in the muscles.
   c. $1.8 \times 21 \times 5 = 189 \text{ dm}^3$
4. Nose, trachea, bronchus, bronchioles, alveoli.

27. Joints in the Human Body

1. a. Shoulder, elbow, wrist.
   b. Shoulder.
2. a. Muscle
   b. By contracting.
3. a. A pair of muscles that work in opposite directions.
   b. Biceps and triceps

28. Plants and Photosynthesis

1. Nitrogen, phosphorus and potassium.
2. Potassium nitrate and sodium phosphate.
3. Higher temperature and more carbon dioxide.
4. a. To get crops earlier which then sell for a higher price. The extra income is greater than the initial costs.
   b. Conditions inside the polytunnel are benefical for plants and pests.
   c. The extra costs are not recovered because the potatoes are sold at a much lower price.
   d. The same plants will use up the same minerals in the soil. If these are not replaced the crops will grow less well.
   Pests and diseases remain in the soil from year to year.